DISCOVER CANADA

Ontario

By Kathryn MacKay

Consultants

Desmond Morton, FRSC, Professor of History, University of Toronto

Gail Stelter, Curriculum Consultant, Halton Roman Catholic School Board

Grolier Limited
TORONTO

Horseshoe Falls and daffodils, Niagara Falls
Overleaf: **Lake Superior and the Sleeping Giant, a huge rock
formation across from Thunder Bay**

Canadian Cataloguing in Publication Data

MacKay, Kathryn E. (Kathryn Elizabeth), 1953-
  Ontario

(Discover Canada)
Rev. ed.
Includes index.
ISBN 0-7172-3136-4

1. Ontario — Juvenile literature. I. Title.
II. Series: Discover Canada (Toronto, Ont.).

FC3061.2.M33 1996   j971.3   C96-9310320-3
F1057.4.M33 1996

Printed and bound in Canada.
Published simultaneously in the United States.
 3 4 5 6 7 8 9 10 DWF 99 98 97 96

Front cover: Fall foliage, Long Lake, Haliburton Highlands
Back cover: Fireworks display, Ontario Place, Toronto

The Parliament Buildings, Ottawa

Table of Contents

CHAPTER 1

Ontario —
Yours to Discover

Welcome to Ontario, a province where "Variety is the spice of life!" Ontario has a wide diversity of landscapes, communities, people and ways of life!

Barren rock, long sandy beaches, grassy meadows and lush woodlands are all to be found in Ontario. Gently rolling farmland lies in the shadow of sheer rock cliffs, slowly gliding rivers turn into thundering waterfalls and tracts of wilderness are tamed to wooded glades. With its open fields, extensive waterways, vast reaches of forest and wildlife that ranges from rattlesnakes and opossums to polar bears, Ontario's scenery has something for everyone.

Ontario's population is equally varied — a true human mosaic. Canada's First Nations have made the province their home for thousands of years. French and British settlers planted roots here over two hundred years ago; since then they have been joined by people from all over the world. All of these people have enriched Ontario with their different languages, skills, religions, customs and crafts.

The people of Ontario follow many ways of life. They live in isolated wilderness areas, in small farming communities, in mid-sized towns, small industrialized cities or the sprawling metropolis of Toronto. They work at farming, mining, or forestry, or in business, industry, or sales. There are real estate developers, transport drivers, bush pilots, manufacturers, artists, computer programmers, students, athletes — people in almost every occupation imaginable.

Ontario is a lively province, full of exciting things to learn, see and do. Read the following pages, and discover a province that is rich with the spice of life.

The boardwalk over Wye Marsh near Penetanguishene

CHAPTER 2

The Land

If you were to draw a line across a map of Ontario from Mattawa in the east to the north end of Lake Huron, you would be marking out the province's two main regions, northern Ontario and southern Ontario. Agriculture, manufacturing and business are the chief occupations in the gentler region of the south, while forestry and mining are the main industries in the harsher region to the north.

Land Area

Ontario covers more than 1 068 000 square kilometres (412 000 square miles), which is almost 11 percent of the whole of Canada. Any European country but Russia could easily fit into it with room to spare for one or two smaller ones. The province measures about 1600 kilometres (1000 miles) at its widest point and just a little more from north to south. It is anything but square, however. Hudson Bay and James Bay take big bites out of its northern edge; in the south, a triangle juts eastward between the Ottawa and St. Lawrence rivers, while the southern tip of the Niagara Peninsula is actually a little south of California's northern border.

Topography and Geography

Ontario shares all three of its main geographical regions — the Canadian Shield, the Hudson Bay Lowland and the Great Lakes-St. Lawrence Lowlands — with its eastern neighbour, Quebec, and the first two with its western neighbour, Manitoba.

Overleaf: **Farm near Magnetawan**

Left: Sunset off the northern shore of Lake Superior. *Right*: Farm near Stayner, west of Barrie

The Canadian Shield, which contains some of the oldest rock in the world, sweeps across the middle two-thirds of Ontario. Its vast, rugged expanses are covered with forest and cradle thousands of lakes.

The Hudson Bay Lowland is a strip of flat, marshy land, scattered with large boulders, that encircles Hudson and James bays. Few people live in this bleak stretch of wilderness, but oddly enough it is the site of the first English settlement in the province, Moose Factory.

South of the Canadian Shield lie the Great Lakes-St. Lawrence Lowlands. This area contains some of the richest farmland in Canada and is home to most of the province's people. The landscape is varied: fringing the shield are forested areas dotted with lakes; much of the rest is rolling country, with flat stretches here and there. The most conspicuous feature is the Niagara Escarpment, a steep limestone ridge that runs northwest from the Niagara River to Lake Huron.

Right: Canadian Shield country. *Far right*: Southern Ontario farmland

The Forests

Ontario's 425 000 square kilometres (164 000 square miles) of forest have always been a valuable natural resource. For thousands of years, the forest provided nearly everything the native peoples needed to survive: the materials with which they built homes and canoes; edible fruits and roots and leaves and bark and mosses for medicine; shelter and food for the animals they hunted.

The four main forests of Ontario are the Niagara Forest, the Great Lakes-St. Lawrence Forest, the Boreal Forest and the Subarctic Forest.

The Niagara Forest is the smallest as well as the most southern. Its main species of trees are maple, beech, basswood, ash, hickory, oak, white pine, red cedar and sumach. This forest also contains some exotic species such as magnolia, chestnut, paw-paw and sassafras.

The Great Lakes-St. Lawrence Forest has been Ontario's main source of lumber. It is a mixed-wood forest with both conifers such as white pine and white spruce, and deciduous trees such as birch,

Left: Aerial view of northwestern Ontario's Boreal Forest. *Above*: Mixed-wood forest once covered southern Ontario, and today's rich farmlands all had to be painstakingly cleared by the pioneers who settled them.

poplar, maple and oak. This forest is thicker in the north, where conifers predominate, than in the south: in the areas of Algonquin Park and Lake Superior, almost 90 percent of the land is covered with trees.

The Boreal Forest contains black spruce, white spruce, tamarack, balsam fir and jack pine. This vast forest stretches from Manitoba to Quebec and provides northern Ontario with its main pulpwood resource.

The Subarctic Forest actually has few trees. It lies in the far north of the province and because of its latitude, it has a very short growing season. As well, the land is poorly drained. A few stands of smallish trees do grow there, but they are rare.

The Water

The name *Ontario* comes from an Iroquoian word that has been variously translated as "shining water," "sparkling water" and "beautiful lake." It was first given to the smallest of the Great Lakes then, at Confederation, to the province. In spite of pollution problems that may make it less descriptive than it once was, it remains an appropriate name for a province that contains almost 177 000 square kilometres (68 000 square miles) of lakes and rivers — over a quarter of the world's supply of fresh water.

Georgian Bay. *Inset*: **Rushing waters at the heart of Algonquin Park**

In addition to its share of four Great Lakes, Ontario has several quite large lakes including Lakes Simcoe, Nipigon, Nipissing and St. Clair, Lake of the Woods, Lac Seul and Rainy Lake, plus an estimated 250 000 more. (Not too surprisingly, no one seems to have managed to make a precise count of them all.) Joining, feeding and draining these lakes are countless large and small rivers. Apart from the well-known St. Lawrence and Ottawa rivers that form the province's southeastern boundaries, the biggest rivers are in northern Ontario. They include the Severn, Winisk, Attawapiskat, Albany, Missinaibi and Moose, which empty into Hudson Bay and James Bay.

This wealth of rivers and lakes was important to the settlement and development of the province. Lakes and rivers were Ontario's original "highways," and natives, explorers, fur traders and settlers travelled by water wherever they could. As the province grew, heavy trees that provided lumber for building could be floated down rivers to settlement areas. The rivers and lakes also provided a constant source of fresh drinking water, as well as power for grist mills, sawmills and other early industries. Later the power of rivers, streams and falls was harnessed to generate electricity.

The hydroelectric power generated from Niagara Falls was particularly important in developing Ontario's manufacturing industries. Niagara Falls ranks third in the world for the volume of water that thunders over its rim — fifteen billion litres (four billion gallons) an hour. Today the falls provide only a fraction of the electricity the province uses, but their spectacular beauty makes them one of the world's natural wonders and attracts tourists from many countries.

Ontario's main waterway is the St. Lawrence Seaway, with its canals and locks. The Seaway is the province's most important transport route for raw materials, crops and manufactured goods. These products are shipped to distant world markets on large ocean-going vessels that can start on their voyages from the head of the Great Lakes, at the heart of Canada.

Above: Fishing at Nestor Falls, at the eastern tip of Lake of the Woods. *Right*: The 43-km (27-mi.) long Welland Canal is a major link in the St. Lawrence Seaway. About 4000 ships pass through the canal each year.

Wildlife

From the huge polar bears roaming the northern shores of Hudson Bay to the squirrels that scurry across Toronto lawns and the raccoons that tip over its garbage cans, Ontario teems with wildlife. Beaver, otter, mink, muskrat, groundhogs, rabbits, skunks, chipmunks, wildcats, wolves, black bears and fox all live in Ontario's forests. Roaming freely in the wilderness are caribou and moose. Deer are common in southern Ontario's "cottage country" as the many deer-crossing signs along secondary roads attest.

Many species of birds fly over and breed in Ontario. In towns and cities, the most common species are pigeons, seagulls, sparrows, crows and robins. In rural areas, hawks, crows, woodpeckers, jays, starlings, chickadees, nuthatches and finches are plentiful. For many people who live in the country, spring and autumn are heralded by the honking of migrating Canada geese as they fly

Wildlife abounds even in heavily populated southern Ontario. *Above left*: Red fox. *Above*: A family of blue jays. *Left*: White-tailed deer

across the sky in perfect V-formation. Cottagers and campers are often moved by the loon's haunting cry at dawn and dusk.

Ontario is also home to many species of snakes (including one venomous one, the massasauga rattler), turtles, frogs and salamanders. The five-lined skink, found at the tip of the Niagara Peninsula, is the only lizard in eastern Canada.

Farmland

Southern Ontario is the most intensively farmed region in Canada.
It supports several types of farms, including beef, dairy, corn, fruit
and mixed produce. South central and southwestern Ontario are
the core farming regions. As these areas are also the most heavily
populated, farmland has come to be threatened by the severing of
lots for housing and industrial development, private estates and
hobby farms. Valuable land is also gradually being covered by the
ever-expanding urban sprawl that surrounds the province's larger
cities. These trends are alarming, as most of the rest of Ontario is
unsuitable for successful farming.

The soil of northern Ontario is rocky, poorly drained, and generally infertile for growing most crops. There are, however, a number
of dairy and beef farms on Manitoulin Island and near Rainy River.
Still, farming remains a minor activity in northern Ontario.

Climate

Given the province's size, it is not surprising that the climate varies
considerably from one place to another. By the time the ice breaks
up on the rivers flowing into Hudson Bay and James Bay, the bright
yellow forsythia blossoms have come and gone in Toronto and the
lilacs are already giving way to roses.

All of Ontario has four distinct seasons: winter, spring, summer
and autumn. Naturally, northern Ontario is generally colder in all
these seasons than southern Ontario. However, places like Kenora
and Timmins can enjoy summer days as hot as those of more south-
erly points because they are away from the cooling effects of the
Great Lakes. In fact, the hottest temperatures ever recorded in the
province, 42.2° C (108° F) in July 1936, were at Atikokan and Fort
Frances, west of Lake Superior. The average January temperature
near Hudson Bay is −25° C (−13° F). The average mid-January
temperature near Lake Ontario is −5° C (23° F). The average

midsummer temperature in the province's far north is 12° C (54° F), while in the south it is 21° C (70° F).

Most of the province receives over 500 millimetres (20 inches) of rainfall a year, with some parts of southern Ontario getting about twice that much. The area east of Lake Huron is known as the Snow Belt, with places like Parry Sound and Midland getting upwards of 300 centimetres (120 inches) of snow a year.

An early snowfall finds autumn leaves still clinging to the trees. *Inset*: The arethusa is a member of the orchid family. Nicknamed "dragon's mouth," it grows in bogs and other moist places.

CHAPTER 3
The First Nations

No one really knows when human beings first made their appearance in what is now Ontario. What we do know is that 20 000 years ago a thick layer of ice covered the entire area (and almost all the rest of Canada as well) so that nothing could live there. Then, probably about 12 000 years ago, this glacier began to melt. As it slowly retreated northward, it left behind land that could again support life. Plants grew, animals moved in, and people followed.

Other than some rock carvings, the meaning of which no one fully understands, the early inhabitants left no written records. What we know of them and their ways of life is therefore based on traditions and stories passed down by word of mouth to their descendants, on the findings of archaeologists and on the writings of the first Europeans who met them.

By the time the first Europeans arrived in the early seventeenth century, several tribes of natives belonging to two main groups were established in the Ontario region. The groups were distinguished by the languages they spoke and their different ways of life. In the north and northwest, were the Ojibwa, Algonquin and Cree, who lived by hunting and gathering and who spoke related Algonkian languages. South and east of Lake Huron were the Huron, Tobacco, Erie and Neutral peoples, who lived mainly by farming. They spoke languages belonging to the Iroquoian language family and were distantly related to the five tribes of the Iroquois Confederacy — the Seneca, Cayuga, Onondaga, Oneida and Mohawk — who lived south of Lake Ontario and the St. Lawrence River in what is now New York State.

Ojibwa encampment on Pie Island in Lake Superior

Both the Algonkians and the Iroquoians lived by making use of the resources of the land around them. Their different ways of life were mainly the result of their adaptation, over centuries, to different physical environments. The Algonkians lived on a land of rock, bush, muskeg, dense forest, lakes and streams. It teemed with wildlife but was not at all suitable for agriculture. The Iroquoians, on the other hand, lived in a well-watered region where the soil was fertile, and where long hot summers gave corn time to ripen.

The Algonkian Way of Life

Algonkians were loosely organized in groups of related families called bands. In winter, the bands divided up the hunting area and each family camped and hunted on its own. The families then gathered again in the spring. Each band had a chief, but decisions were usually made by general discussion and agreement.

Hunting was the Algonkians' most important activity. They hunted moose, elk, caribou and deer with bows and arrows. Traps and snares were set to catch smaller animals such as beaver and rabbits. These animals provided not only much of their food, but also skins for clothing, sinew for sewing and bowstrings, and bones for making tools and utensils.

To add to their diet, the Algonkians used nets, hooks, harpoons, spears and traps to catch the fish that abounded in the many lakes and rivers of their northern region. Women gathered nuts, berries, mushrooms and edible roots, and harvested wild rice in areas where it grew. In early spring, they tapped maple trees and made syrup from the sap.

The Algonkians had to move often in search of the animals they hunted, so they needed homes that were either easily portable or that they could build anywhere with commonly found materials. In fact, the Algonkians made a compromise: to raise a house, they built a frame by binding saplings into either a cone or a dome shape and covering the frame with animal skins, pieces of bark or mats

Algonkian women share the tasks involved in collecting the sap from maple trees and boiling it down to make syrup and sugar.

made of rushes. When a family had to move, it packed up the wigwam's covering and left the poles behind.

In summer, the Algonkians travelled mainly by canoe. Birch bark was the favourite material for covering canoes, but in areas where birch was scarce, they used elm or spruce bark. Bark canoes were rather fragile, but they had two big advantages: they were light and so they were easy to carry when necessary, and the material for repairing them was always at hand. In winter, the Algonkians travelled on foot, using snowshoes of various designs — wide and rounded for soft snow, narrow and with pointed ends for hard snow.

The Iroquoian Way of Life

The Iroquoian peoples who lived in what is now southern Ontario seem to have begun growing crops of corn about 100 B.C. Four hundred years later, they were also growing beans and squash and tobacco. The men of the tribes used stone tools to clear patches of land of trees and scrub. The women used tools made of sharp animal bones, such as the shoulder-blades of moose, to break up the clumps of earth and pointed sticks to push seeds into the soil. It was the women, too, who tended the crops as they grew, harvested

Guarding the cornfields — Iroquoian women make noise to scare birds away from the ripening crops. *Inset*: The interior of a longhouse

them when they were ready, and dried and stored them for winter. They also gathered berries and other wild plants and made maple syrup in the spring.

Iroquoian men hunted and fished to add to their food stocks and to get skins for clothing. They mainly used the same types of fishing and hunting gear as the Algonkians.

Because the Iroquoians could grow much of their food, they could live a more settled life than their Algonkian neighbours, moving only when they had used up all the wood available nearby, or when the ground became infertile from too much cultivation. For the same reason, they could build bigger houses and many people could live together in villages.

An Iroquoian village was made up of a cluster of large communal dwellings called longhouses. These were made by covering a tunnel-shaped framework of saplings with pieces of thick bark. Down the centre inside was an open space, and in the middle of the space, a row of open cooking fires. Holes were left in the roof above the fires to allow the smoke to escape. (Unfortunately, too little of it did and it was common for older people to become blind.) Along both sides of the longhouse was a row of sleeping platforms curtained off with animal skins.

Most of these villages had a special longhouse used for community meetings, at which plans were made and problems were solved by discussion. As well, most were surrounded by a palisade of poles, for protection against enemies. The fields were outside the palisade.

The World of Spirit

Both the Algonkians and the Iroquoians shared the belief that there was a soul, or spirit, in everything in nature: people, animals, trees, rocks, rivers, the sun, moon and stars, and the weather. They believed too, that spirits were a source of power and that it was important to respect that power. This meant living as far as possible in harmony with nature, giving thanks for all good things and sharing with one another.

Besides the spirit in each natural object there was the Great Spirit, the Creator, who was all-powerful. In addition, both these groups of natives believed that each person, at the age of about thirteen or fourteen, could receive a guardian spirit or helper. To receive such a spirit young boys and some young girls went into the woods to fast and pray. They expected — and usually experienced — a vivid dream. They would return to the village and tell this dream to the *shaman* (medicine man), who would interpret its meaning. This experience was an important part of growing up and taking one's place in adult society.

CHAPTER 4
A Brief History

The first Europeans who journeyed deep into the heartland of North America came with high hopes. Some adventurers were looking for the Western Sea, of which the natives had told them, in hopes that it might be the fabled Northwest Passage that would lead to the wealth of Asia. Others hoped to claim land where they could set up new colonies to enrich their homeland. Some came as missionaries, hoping to convert the natives to their own Christian beliefs. Still others planned to become wealthy by trading for furs.

The French were the first Europeans to reach the area that would become Ontario. In 1608, Samuel de Champlain established a settlement at Quebec on the lower St. Lawrence River, and thus founded the colony of New France. From this base, he sent out men to explore the interior of the country. One of those sent out was a seventeen-year-old lad named Etienne Brulé, whose mission was to live for a time with the Hurons and learn their ways. Brulé adapted quickly to the life and was probably the first European to see Lakes Ontario, Erie and Huron. In 1613, and again in 1615, Brulé guided Champlain into the Great Lakes region and introduced him to the Hurons. An alliance was formed, and for the next thirty years, the Hurons would serve as middlemen in the French fur trade, providing a link between the French and the Algonkian tribes in the fur-rich country farther north.

Jesuit missionaries arrived in Canada soon after the first explorers, eager to convert the Hurons to Christianity. To this end they built a mission near the present town of Midland on the southwest

Pioneer family in the Upper Canadian wilderness

shore of Georgian Bay. But contact with Europeans exposed the natives to diseases that were new and therefore highly dangerous to them. In 1638 an epidemic of smallpox killed about half the tribe. Ten years later the rest of the Huron villages were destroyed by Iroquois warriors who wanted to control the fur trade and who had obtained guns from Dutch traders. The few surviving Hurons scattered, some to the west or south, a small group to other settlements of New France. The Iroquois then proceeded to attack and disperse all the other native tribes in what is now southern Ontario.

The Fur Trade

After the Huron villages and the Jesuit missions were destroyed, the French limited their settlements west of Montreal to trading

Life at the Jesuit missions in the 1640s is recreated at Sainte-Marie Among the Hurons. The reconstruction includes a palisade, a church and several other buildings in addition to the longhouse and workshop seen here.

posts. They ran a flourishing trade through the late 1600s from their main post of Fort Cataraqui (later Fort Frontenac, now Kingston). From this post and others, French explorers including Robert Cavelier de La Salle, Louis Jolliet and Father Marquette ventured across the Great Lakes and down the Mississippi River, through the heart of the continent.

Two particularly colourful French fur traders were Pierre Radisson and his brother-in-law, Médard Chouart des Groseilliers. Unhappy with the way they were treated by the governor of New France, Radisson and Groseilliers offered their services to the English. The result was the creation of the Hudson's Bay Company under a Royal Charter that gave the company control of all the land that drained into Hudson Bay. One of the first forts built in Rupert's Land, as this vast area was called, was Moose Factory on the western shore of James Bay.

The French, of course, felt no great need to respect English royal charters and so they built a few posts of their own on the northern bays. A number of battles ensued, forts changed hands a few times, and then finally, in 1713, the French acknowledged once and for all English title to Rupert's Land.

Moose Factory was built by the Hudson's Bay Company in 1673 on an island at the mouth of the Moose River.

This meant that French traders had to seek new sources of furs. In the 1730s Pierre Gaultier de La Vérendrye and his sons began a series of expeditions west of Lake Superior that eventually took them into present-day Saskatchewan. In all, they built eight trading posts between Saskatchewan and the St. Lawrence River, opening up the land west of Lake Superior to the fur trade. They established the first of these trading posts in 1731, near what is now Fort Frances. Their main fort was Fort St. Charles, on the northwest corner of Lake of the Woods. Although Indians attacked and destroyed this fort in 1763, the town of Kenora grew from the first settlement there.

Fur trade competition continued even after France lost its North American colony in 1763. Now it was mainly Scottish merchants, based in Montreal, who sent traders along La Vérendrye's route to the far northwest. In 1774, a number of small fur-trading operations joined forces to form the North West Company. Now that they were not competing with each other as well as with the Hudson's Bay Company, the Nor'Westers, as they were called, could devote their attention and resources to streamlining their operations. Their system of exchanging supplies for furs midway between Montreal and their western outposts gave birth to a thriving community at Fort William (now part of Thunder Bay). And in 1799 the company built a canoe lock for their freighter canoes at Sault Ste. Marie, thus connecting Lakes Huron and Superior. Today Sault Ste. Marie has one of the busiest canal systems on the St. Lawrence Seaway.

Early Wars

Three wars played a major role in creating Ontario and in determining the make-up of its population and the character of its people.

The Seven Years' War was a war made in Europe, waged by several European powers and fought on three continents. But its long-term impact was probably as great in North America as it was anywhere. Under the terms of the Treaty of Paris, which officially ended the war in 1763, France gave up the lands in North America

that had been known as New France. This meant that Canada —
including Ontario — would develop as a British, not a French
colony.

In 1774, the British Parliament passed the Quebec Act, which re-
organized their recently acquired territory. Part of what is now
Ontario and the large area between the Ohio and Mississippi rivers
were annexed to the new colony of Quebec. The act also allowed
the people of Quebec to keep their Roman Catholic religion, their
language and French civil law. There would be no elected assembly
as there was in the older British colonies, and a British governor
would direct Quebec's affairs.

The people of Britain's older American colonies were outraged.
Some were offended by the concessions to the Catholic church,
others by the lack of an elected assembly. Most viewed Quebec's
control of the Ohio territory as an intolerable restriction on their
freedom to expand. The Quebec Act thus became one of the many
grievances that resulted in the American War of Independence.

Although most American colonists resented some aspects of British treatment of them, not all felt that independence was a better
alternative. For various reasons, many chose to remain loyal to the
British Crown. As early as 1776, after the American Declaration of
Independence, some of these people headed north to Quebec,
which was firmly under British control. More stayed behind, however — some to fight for Britain, others simply unwilling to
abandon their homes as long as there was a chance the rebels
would lose the war.

Loyalists, as those Americans who sided with the British were
called, trickled into Quebec throughout the war. In 1783, the Treaty
of Paris officially recognized the United States of America as an in-
dependent nation, and the trickle became a flood. By winter, there
were about 7000 Loyalist refugees camped along the St. Lawrence
west of Montreal, waiting to be resettled.

The colonial government had already decided what to do with
them — send them west to open up the lands between the Great

Above: Loyalist encampment near present-day Kingston. *Inset*: A Loyalist choosing the "ticket" that will specify the location of the land he will get. *Right*: The Mohawk Village on the Grand River Reserve. The church, built in 1785, was the first Protestant church in Upper Canada. Known as Her Majesty's Chapel of the Mohawks, it can still be seen near Brantford.

Lakes and the Ottawa River. Surveyors were dispatched to divide up some of the land along the upper St. Lawrence into townships and farmlots. Meanwhile, the Loyalists had to be equipped, since most had arrived with little more than the clothes on their backs.

Each family was given a tent, clothes for three years and food rations; an axe and a hoe were provided for each man and one musket for hunting to every five men; seeds were distributed to be divided up among the members of a community. Individuals drew "location tickets" from a hat telling them which piece of land would be theirs.

Among the refugees were many men who had fought with Loyalist regiments. It was decided to settle these men and their families in blocks, according to their regiment, for purposes of defence. Among them also were two groups of Loyalist Mohawk Indians led by chiefs Joseph Brant and John Deseronto. Brant and his group were given a large grant of land along the Grand River north of Lake Erie. The smaller Deseronto group chose to settle on the Bay of Quinte.

For a while, most Loyalists were too busy turning bush and forest into farms and homes to worry much about anything else. Within a few years, however, they were agitating for political change. They did not like living under French civil law, especially since the land tenure system did not give individuals absolute ownership of land. They wanted to own their land, they wanted the laws they were used to and they wanted an elected assembly.

In order to satisfy them without upsetting the French population too much, the British Parliament passed the Constitutional Act in 1791. This act divided Quebec into Upper Canada, which later became Ontario, and Lower Canada, which later regained its earlier name of Quebec. Both would get an elected assembly, but otherwise Lower Canada would remain much as it had been. The Loyalists would get the English laws and land system they were used to.

Colonel John Graves Simcoe, who had commanded a Loyalist regiment during the war, was appointed Upper Canada's first lieutenant-governor. He arrived in 1792 and immediately saw that what Upper Canada needed most was more people. To attract settlers, he began granting large tracts of land to individuals who promised to settle it. He had roads built, and he saw to it that the availability of good, free farmland was widely publicized in the United States. This brought in thousands of Americans, sometimes called "Late Loyalists," and by 1812, Upper Canada had a population of over 80 000.

The War of 1812

To a certain extent, the War of 1812, like the North American phase of the Seven Years' War, was a result of conflict in Europe. Britain was again embroiled in a major war with France — this time against the Emperor Napoleon whose ambition was to rule all of Europe. To prevent supplies from reaching France, the British began stopping and searching all neutral ships — most of which were American. While they were at it, they arrested anyone they thought was a deserter from the Royal Navy, and occasionally they seized American sailors by mistake. This interference with their trade and their citizens enraged the Americans, who had other grievances against Britain as well. In particular, they were convinced that the British had been helping the Indians of the Ohio Territory in their efforts to stop American settlers from taking over their lands.

"Warhawks" in the United States Congress wanted something done about all those things, and in 1812 they got their way: the United States declared war on Britain. Taking Upper Canada was the obvious first step. It would be an easy target, everyone was

The Battle of Queenston Heights, October 13, 1812. Today, a 56-m (184-ft.) monument towers over the battle site, commemorating the British-Canadian victory. General Isaac Brock, who was mortally wounded in the battle, is buried beneath the monument.

sure; its population was tiny — and most of them were Americans anyway — and Britain had few soldiers or resources to spare to defend it.

Full of confidence, the Americans launched their attack across the Detroit River — and got a surprise. Under the command of Major General Isaac Brock, a small number of British regulars, Canadian militia, and Shawnee Indians led by Tecumseh, seized the American fort of Michilimackinac, pushed the Americans back across the Detroit River and then took Detroit. A few weeks later they repelled a major attack across the Niagara River at Queenston.

The death of Tecumseh, October 5, 1813

The battle at Queenston was a splendid victory but a costly one: Brock was killed during the fighting. He died not knowing that he had been knighted for his victory at Detroit. Just a few days short of a year later, Tecumseh was killed at the Battle of Moraviantown.

Through 1813 and 1814, the war continued. Naval battles on Lake Erie went mainly to the Americans, but the British retained control of Lake Ontario. Meanwhile, land battles went both ways. One of them, at Beaver Dam, produced a Canadian heroine, Laura Secord, who walked thirty kilometres (twenty miles) through fields and woods to warn the British of a planned American attack.

The Treaty of Ghent officially ended the war on December 24, 1814. Each side returned the territory it had seized, and the boundaries remained unchanged. Nevertheless, the war had important effects on Upper Canada. Immigration patterns changed: American immigration naturally stopped during the war and was discouraged for some time afterward, and many of the soldiers who had been sent to defend the province chose to stay on as settlers. Loyalties were also sorted out: some post-Loyalist settlers from the

United States went back during or after the war; most stayed, and they and the rest of Upper Canada's immigrant population became aware that this land was now their home and they were ready to defend it.

Rebellion, Reform and Responsible Government

In 1791, the Loyalists got the elected assembly they wanted, but that did not mean that Upper Canada had a truly democratic government. As well as the assembly, there were two councils, both appointed, and a governor sent from Britain. The governor made the final decisions, and nothing obliged him to pay much attention to the assembly's wishes. More often than not he preferred to be guided by the councils, which were dominated by a small, close-knit group of people nicknamed the Family Compact. These people tended to be wealthy, Anglican and conservative in their views.

In time, as the province grew and the composition of the population changed, many Upper Canadians came to resent this situation and began to elect "oppositionists" — people who would try to change it — to the assembly. Two of the most prominent oppositionists, or reformers, in the 1820s and 1830s were William Lyon Mackenzie and Robert Baldwin.

Mackenzie, a Scottish immigrant, founded a journal called *The Colonial Advocate* and used it to attack the Family Compact. He was elected to the assembly in 1828, and over the next few years, his sharp tongue got him thrown out five times. Each time he was re-elected and in 1834 he became Toronto's first mayor. Mackenzie was not a patient man, and by 1837 he had become bitter about the failure of reformist efforts to get changes made. He organized some fellow-radicals, mostly farmers from north of Toronto, and staged a rebellion. It was a miserable failure, and Mackenzie fled to the United States, where he stayed for eleven years.

The Mackenzie rebellion, along with one in Lower Canada, did succeed in catching British attention, however. A new governor,

The Battle of Montgomery's Tavern, the main battle of the 1837 rebellion in Upper Canada. *Inset, left to right*: William Lyon Mackenzie, Robert Baldwin, Lord Durham

Lord Durham, was specifically instructed to investigate the causes of the discontent and come up with solutions. His report recommended uniting the two colonies and establishing a *responsible* government — that is a government run by people who were members of the elected assembly and who stayed in office only as long as they had the support of a majority of the elected representatives.

The first of these recommendations was accepted, and in 1841 the Act of Union came into effect, creating the United Province of Canada. Upper Canada officially became Canada West and Lower

The Battle of Ridgeway, fought near Fort Erie in 1866, was an attack by a group of Irish-American extremists called Fenians, who felt that their best chance of hurting England was to invade Canada. The attack was quickly dispersed, but the threat posed by the Fenians helped the Confederation movement.

Canada, Canada East, though the old names continued in general use. Responsible government was a few more years in coming, and it came largely as a result of the efforts of Robert Baldwin. Elected to the assembly in the late 1820s, Baldwin was a moderate reformer who was not in favour of Mackenzie's rebellion. He was defeated in 1830 and not re-elected until after the Union. He soon became the leader of Canada West's reformers and formed an alliance with Louis Hippolyte LaFontaine, his counterpart in Canada East. Together, mostly as an opposition party, they pressed for responsible government and finally won a sweeping victory allowing them to establish it in 1848.

Confederation and the Early Premiers

During the 1860s, the government of the United Province of Canada often found itself in a state of deadlock. Conservatives, a minority in Canada West but a majority in Canada East, about balanced out the Reformers (known by now as Grits, later as Liberals) and nothing much could get done. Partly as a result of this situation, four provinces of British North America decided to join together to form a new country. The British Parliament passed the British North America Act (now known as the Constitution Act, 1867) and on July 1, 1867, the Dominion of Canada was born.

The new country had four provinces: Ontario, Quebec, New Brunswick and Nova Scotia. John A. Macdonald, the colourful lawyer from Kingston who had headed the Union government for several years and who had pushed hard for Confederation, became Canada's first prime minister.

Two weeks later, John Sandfield Macdonald became the first premier of Ontario. He carried on with the agenda of the previous government, framing laws relating to education, roads, railways, social policy and property and civil rights.

In 1872, Oliver Mowat led the Liberal Party to victory and remained premier for almost twenty-four years.

In 1878, Mowat began to fight for a new western boundary for Ontario that angled southwestward along the Albany River from James Bay to where the Winnipeg River crosses the present-day Manitoba-Ontario border. The federal government and, later, Manitoba opposed Ontario's claim, and the dispute was finally settled in 1889, in Ontario's favour, gaining the province another 233 000 square kilometres (90 000 square miles). "New Ontario" — as this region was called — contained a wealth of natural resources but very poor agricultural land.

During Mowat's years of office, Ontario's mining, hydroelectric power and forestry industries all began to develop into the major industries they are today. One reason for their early success was Sir John A. Macdonald's "National Policy." From 1879, this policy protected Ontario's industries by imposing high tariffs on imported goods to make them more expensive than made-in-Ontario products.

After more than thirty years of Liberal government, the Conservative Party, led by James P. Whitney, was elected in Ontario in 1905. Whitney's government founded the Ontario Hydro-Electric Commission. This publicly owned utility was steered by then cabinet minister Adam Beck, a strong-willed man determined to provide affordable electricity for the people of Ontario. Under his guidance, the utility grew rapidly, just keeping pace with the industrial development that cheap electricity promoted.

The 1900s

The First World War began in August 1914. Because the war demanded equipment and men, it affected Ontario as well as the rest of the country. The province's factories almost doubled in size to churn out hundreds of thousands of vehicles and other supplies. As men were going off by the thousands to the battlefields of Europe, women filled many of the positions that were opening in industry and business.

For years, many Ontario women had been demanding more rights, including the right to vote. The war gave them their chance.

Scenes of Ontario life at the turn of the century

As more and more women joined the paid workforce, attitudes toward women changed. Ontario's Premier Hearst suddenly announced in 1917 that women would be given the vote in the next provincial election — and they were. Later in the same year, the prime minister, Sir Robert Borden, who needed support for his bill introducing military conscription, announced that women in Canada's military services and the wives, mothers and sisters of Canadian servicemen could vote in the up-coming federal election. In 1919, that right was extended to all Canadian women.

Before the 1917 federal election, Sir Robert Borden had assured Canada's farmers that conscription would not apply to rural areas where the population was already dropping. A few months later he broke his campaign promise. The farmers of Ontario banded together, perhaps because they distrusted the existing political parties, and because they were concerned about the survival of rural communities. They formed a party of their own, and in 1919 they overturned the Conservative government and elected the United Farmers of Ontario.

The 1920s were a decade of change. Ontario boomed and firms that manufactured automobiles, newsprint, appliances and radios all prospered. Suddenly, the boom turned to bust and the 1930s found the world — Ontario included — plunged into the Great Depression. In 1933, Ontario saw lay-offs, bankruptcies, government relief, and the introduction of a provincial income tax. In 1934, the Liberal Party, under Mitchell F. Hepburn, was elected to rescue Ontario from its economic distress. But the general public, battered by financial strains, no longer looked to their province for leadership, but rather to the federal government. Tragically, it took the outbreak of the Second World War to bring the Depression to an end.

In 1939, Canada declared war on Germany after that country had invaded Austria, Czechoslovakia and Poland. The Second World War brought Ontario investment, employment, industry, technology and shortages. Civilians accepted the rationing of gasoline,

Top: Bay Street, Toronto, in 1924. *Above*: The women of the University of Toronto's 1928 graduating class. *Left*: Government agents dump kegs of homebrew seized in a raid on a "blind pig" (illegal bar) in Elk Lake.

electricity, clothing and some foods as part of their contribution to the war effort. The war ended in 1945, just after the United States dropped the world's first two atomic bombs on Japan.

From 1943 until 1985 Ontario's Conservative Party governed the province through mainly prosperous times. In 1985, the party's long tenure ended when the Liberals under David Peterson, formed first a minority then a majority government. In 1990, the New Democratic Party, led by Bob Rae, won power for the first time in Ontario, but ceded it to the Conservatives five years later.

CHAPTER 5
The People

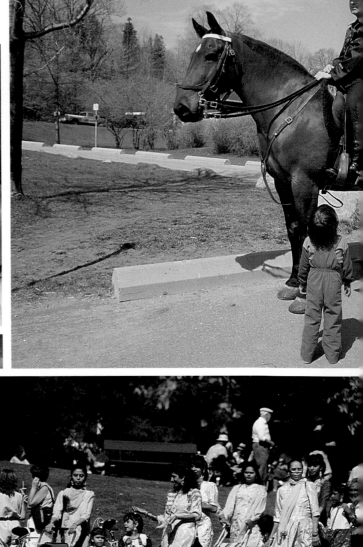

Ontario has always been one of the fastest-growing provinces in Canada. In 1861, it had just under a million and a half people, and 130 years later, it had just over ten million. During all of these years it has represented close to 30 percent of Canada's total population.

Pioneering Times

Ontario's early pioneers had to start from scratch. A simple "lean-to" of poles and brush was often their only shelter for a few weeks as they began the back-breaking job of clearing enough land of trees and rocks to build a simple log cabin. This cabin would be home for the two or three years it usually took to build a more comfortable house.

The pioneers sowed and reaped their first crops among the tree stumps. Gradually, they cleared their land, built fences, dug and planted gardens, made furniture and added to their livestock. The women and girls tended the gardens, prepared and stored food, wove blankets, stitched clothes, made candles and did all they could to make their homes more secure and comfortable.

When the family could afford it, they built a new and larger home and the first log cabin became a storage shed or a pigsty. Neighbours helped one another as they could in times of crisis. Communities built churches and schools — often, at first, just small log buildings. All the men were required to help build and maintain roads. Pioneering was hard and often lonely work, but over the years, most families prospered.

Top left: Guelph in 1830, three years after it was founded by settlement promoter John Galt. *Left*: York, seen here in 1830, would change its name to Toronto and be incorporated as a city four years later. *Above*: The road between Kingston and York

Immigration

Through the early 1800s, the British government continued to use a system of land grants to attract settlers to Upper Canada. The early settlements had been close to British forts and they spread out, first along the waterways and then inland from there. After the War of 1812, as after the American Revolution, groups of army veterans sometimes settled together so that they could help protect the province in case of an attack by the Americans. Thus, men from the

The contrasting lives of rich and poor Torontonians in the late 1800s

same regiments, who had fought for Britain in Europe or America — German Lutherans, for instance, or Roman Catholic Highlanders — were often assigned land in particular townships, where they carried on their own traditions and their own language.

Some of these early communities thrived, while others did not. Groups of Irish and Scottish settlers for example, were granted land in a part of Lanark County where the soil was very poor. The settlers struggled to farm their land for a number of years, but by the 1830s, almost all their communities had disappeared. In contrast, in 1823 Peter Robinson was directed by the government to settle 2000 Irish immigrants just north of Rice Lake. This community

Amherstburg's Emancipation Day Parade, August 1, 1894. The town, an important "terminus" on the Underground Railroad, still celebrates the day the British Empire abolished slavery.

did well in the attractive and fertile area, and was the beginning of the successful town of Peterborough. In the 1830s, two English-women, Susanna Moodie and her sister Catherine Parr Traill, settled in the area and wrote books about the region and their pioneering experiences. These and other published accounts of life in the Canadian "backwoods" were very popular in England and may have encouraged emigration.

Not all settlers who came to Upper Canada in the early 1800s were British. A group of German-speaking Mennonites who wished to settle where they could live apart from the influences of other communities came from Pennsylvania. They were farm people who needed large tracts of land. To buy property as cheaply as possible, they settled inland, near the site of the present city of Kitchener-Waterloo. Theirs was the only early Ontario settlement of any size that was not located near water.

Towards the mid-1800s, people from more remote countries began to arrive in Upper Canada. Jews, Eastern Europeans, Chinese and Italians settled in Toronto, Hamilton and the province's mild southwest area. Some of these people were seeking better economic opportunities for themselves and their children; others were seeking freedom from political oppression and religious persecution. Many Black Americans who had been born into slavery travelled north to freedom in Canada with the help of a secret organization called the Underground Railroad. They settled in towns such as St. Catharines, Chatham and Dresden, in Great Lakes ports such as Toronto, Owen Sound or Collingwood, or in the Queen's Bush, unclaimed land lying north of the better farmland of the southwestern region of the province.

During the twentieth century, immigrants have come to Ontario from Asia, India, Europe, the West Indies and the United States. Over time, the percentages from these areas have changed — in the mid-1900s, most immigrants to Ontario came from Europe; now most come from Asia. Destinations have changed as well — whereas once most immigrants fanned out across the province creating new farms, villages and towns, most now choose to settle in Toronto and other major cities of southern Ontario.

A Cultural Mosaic

Ontario's population is now a mosaic of nationalities representing more than seventy countries. Immigrants from almost anywhere can find a community with the same roots somewhere in Ontario. Place names like London, Perth, Dublin and Stratford, Paris and Limoges, Brussels, Dresden, New Hamburg and Odessa testify to the varied origins of the province's people. In Toronto there are neighbourhoods where street names appear in Chinese, Greek or Italian as well as in English, and signs in shop windows are liable to be in any language from Hungarian to Hindi, Spanish to Sinhalese.

At present, just over half of Ontario's population is of British descent. Many of these people treasure family traditions of pioneering days in the province and take pride in Ontario's history of British efforts to settle and protect the land.

The second-largest ethnic group in Ontario is the French commu-

Above: Entertainers at Ottawa's annual Franco-Ontarian Festival. *Left*: The town of Cobourg, founded as a Loyalist settlement, celebrates its birthday. *Below*: Mennonites at St. Jacobs, in the Kitchener-Waterloo area. *Below left*: Asian shopping district in Toronto

Native celebrations featuring elaborate costumes, dance competitions and a wide variety of other events are held in many communities across the province.

nity. Although Franco-Ontarians make up only about 5.5 percent of the population, their ancestors were the original explorers of the province, and its first European settlers. In the later 1800s, French Canadians immigrated into Ontario's eastern and northeastern regions, where most Franco-Ontarians still live today.

Ontario's third largest ethnic group is its Italian community. In the late 1800s, some Italians who were dissatisfied with conditions in their newly unified country left their homeland to seek a better life in Ontario. A second wave of Italians arrived in Toronto after the Second World War, making that city the largest Italian centre in Canada. The next-largest groups are the Chinese and the Germans.

Native Indians now make up only a tiny percentage of Ontario's population. Some 59 000 (a little more than half) live on the province's 197 reserves. The rest live in settlements on Crown land or in towns and cities, with an estimated 20 000 to 30 000 in Metropolitan Toronto.

Ontario's wide variety of peoples practise many different religions. Living in harmony are Roman Catholics, Baptists,

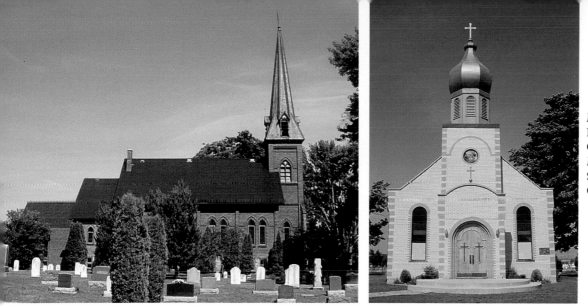

Far left: St. Matthew's Lutheran Church, St. Jacobs. *Left*: St. George Serbian Orthodox Church, Waterloo

Methodists, Lutherans, Mormons, Sikhs, Hindus, Mennonites, Jews, Muslims, Amish and Anglicans, to name just a few religious groups. The province prides itself on its tolerance of and respect for each person's religious beliefs.

Population Distribution

About 90 percent of the province's population lives in southern Ontario, mainly in the area known as the Golden Horseshoe and in cities such as Windsor, Sarnia, London, Kitchener-Waterloo, Kingston and Ottawa. The Golden Horseshoe is the highly industrialized area that borders the northwestern shore of Lake Ontario — from Oshawa to St. Catharines. Home to half of Ontario's population, it includes Toronto — Canada's largest city with a population of over three million — as well as Hamilton and a number of smaller cities and towns.

Even in sparsely populated northern Ontario, most people live in towns and cities, the majority of which are located along railway lines. The largest cities are Sudbury, Thunder Bay, Sault Ste. Marie, North Bay and Timmins. Some smaller communities in northern Ontario can be reached only by air or water — these include Big Trout Lake, Landsdowne House, Fort Hope, Pikangikum and Winisk.

CHAPTER 6

Industrial Growth

Ontario's first industries were fishing, trapping, making potash (from the ashes of the trees the early settlers burned when they cleared their land), farming, forestry and mining. These are called primary industries because they depend directly on natural resources. The raw materials they produce are sold for processing into manufactured goods.

Except for making potash, these industries are still alive in Ontario. Fishing and especially trapping have declined a great deal in importance, however. While they are still a significant source of income to some communities, they now represent only a tiny fraction of one percent of the total value of the province's economic activity. Agriculture, forestry and mining together represent only about 4 percent, but they remain important to the province's economy because they feed its major component — manufacturing.

Ontario is the leading manufacturing province in Canada and has been since before Confederation. It employs just under half of those who work in the country's manufacturing industries and produces just over half the finished products.

Early Influences

Three main factors moulded early Ontario into an industrial leader: the waterways, the railways and the widespread access to hydro-electric power.

Robotic welding line at the General Motors plant, Oshawa

Left: A nineteenth-century observer called cutting away a log jam "one of the most daring feats a lumberman can perform." *Right*: Going through the Welland Canal

As Upper Canada grew, so did the need to improve its transportation routes. Travel by water through the Great Lakes and along the St. Lawrence was certainly faster than travel by land, but it had its problems. At several places, rapids and waterfalls made it necessary to unload goods and passengers, move them overland and then reload them on another vessel. The Welland Canal, completed in 1829, was built to provide a route around Niagara Falls so that ships could get from Lake Ontario to Lake Erie.

The Rideau Canal, which connects the Ottawa River with Lake Ontario, was built between 1826 and 1832 under the direction of Colonel John By of Britain's Royal Engineers. Its purpose was mainly military. After the War of 1812, the government felt that the St. Lawrence was too vulnerable to attack by the Americans. The

A view of Bytown. Named after Lieutenant-Colonel John By, the town was renamed Ottawa in 1855 and became the capital of the United Province of Canada in 1858.

Rideau waterway would provide a safer route for moving troops and supplies should there ever be another war with the United States. The government may have hoped the canal would also have commercial value since it offered a way of avoiding rapids near Cornwall on the St. Lawrence. It was not popular with travellers and merchants, however, because it took so long. Construction was therefore begun on the Cornwall Canal in 1834. Once it was completed, in 1843, products of Upper Canada could at last be quickly and efficiently transported to eastern and overseas markets.

At least for seven months of the year they could. But come mid-November or so, Canada's rivers began to freeze up, and the movement of goods came to an almost complete halt. For this reason, if for no other, Upper Canadians (and Lower Canadians too) greeted the arrival of railways with wild enthusiasm.

Ontario's first railway was the Great Western, originally planned to run from Niagara Falls to Windsor. After many delays, the first stretch of line, between Hamilton and Niagara Falls, opened in 1853. A year later, the line was complete to Windsor. Over the next few years, several extensions were added, reaching Toronto and

Above: A crowd gathers in London, Canada West, to celebrate the official opening of the Great Western Railway in 1853. *Right*: On March 19, 1859, a trestle on the Great Western line near Dundas gave way under the weight of a passing train. Seven people were killed.

points on the shores of Lakes Huron and Erie. The Grand Trunk Railway was a much more ambitious project, meant to link cities on the Great Lakes with Halifax. By 1859 its line ran from Sarnia, through Toronto, to Quebec City, Rivière du Loup and Portland, Maine, and was the longest railway in the world.

These and the many small lines that soon fanned out across southern Ontario opened new land for settlement, creating new markets. They also created a demand for fuel and iron and steel, and for factories to turn out everything from rails and locomotives to spikes and glass windows for passenger cars. In the 1880s, the

This picture gives some idea of the difficulties involved in pushing the Canadian Pacific Railway line through the rugged country north of Lake Superior.

building of Canada's first transcontinental line, the Canadian Pacific Railway, benefitted Ontario in all these ways — and in others as well. During construction, nickel was discovered near Sudbury, spurring the exploration and development of the mineral resources of the Canadian Shield. And by opening the Canadian West for settlement, the CPR helped create a huge new market for Ontario goods.

Later, in the early 1900s, construction of the Temiskaming and Northern Ontario (now called the Ontario Northland) Railway led to the discovery of rich silver deposits near Cobalt. As the line progressed northward from there, more deposits were discovered, of silver, gold, copper and nickel.

Access to relatively cheap hydroelectric power became a major factor in Ontario's growth in the early 1900s. Electricity was around before that — in 1885 Ottawa became the first city in the world to have all its streets lit by electricity — but most of it was generated by wood- or coal-burning steam engines. In the late 1880s, small hydroelectric plants were opened near factories in Ottawa, Peterborough and Georgetown. But the big step came with the development of the huge power potential of Niagara Falls. Transmission from the Falls began in 1903. Three years later, Sir Adam Beck was the driving force in setting up a publicly owned company to supply electricity at cost to Ontario industries and homes. This company, now called Ontario Hydro, has become one of the world's greatest power companies. The affordable electric power it provides added enormously to Ontario's industrial growth.

Farming

In the days of Upper Canada, farming was the most common way of life for the people of Ontario. The early settlers planted patches of potatoes, grain and vegetables, and set out fruit trees so that they would have food to eat. Then, a pioneering family built barns and stables, and raised hens, pigs, cows and sheep. These animals and the crops the fields and garden produced, ensured the pioneers' survival.

Over time, market and service centres were established and grew into towns and cities. More and more newcomers found work there, as did some farmers whose land was not very productive. Those who stayed on the land cleared more fields, planted bigger crops and sold their surplus to feed the growing urban population or for export to Britain and other places.

As farming techniques and machinery improved, it took fewer and fewer farmers to produce ever increasing amounts of food. Around the time of Confederation, over 75 percent of Ontarians lived in rural areas; today only 17 percent do. Nonetheless, and although agriculture accounts for only 2 percent of the province's gross product, Ontario is Canada's biggest agricultural producer. In 1990 it accounted for more than a quarter of the country's total farm production.

Wheat was originally the province's main cash crop. Gradually, and especially after the prairies were settled, wheat gave way to much more diversified farming. Ontario's most important crops are hay, oats, mixed grains and corn. Over the past decade corn, used mostly for feeding livestock, has become the main crop grown in southern Ontario.

Specialty farms developed quite early. After the province's first cheese factory opened in Oxford County in 1864, and its first creamery in Bruce County ten years later, nearby farmers began importing dairy stock. During the first half of the twentieth century, dairy farming was the fastest-growing type of farming. Now it represents about 25 percent of Ontario farm production. Altogether, about two-thirds of the income from farming comes from livestock raised for meat and for eggs and dairy products.

Some regions in Ontario are known for their specialty farms. The Niagara region has been famous for over a century for its peaches,

Far left: Picking peaches in the Niagara area. *Left*: Baling straw on a southwestern Ontario farm. *Below*: Pumpkin field in Prince Edward County

Far right: Shearing sheep on a farm near Bowmanville. *Right*: The celery harvest in the Holland Marsh

grapes and other fruit. Four marshes in southern Ontario — Holland, Thedford, Erieau and Pelee — have been drained, and vegetables are now grown there. Canning tomatoes are grown in Essex County and apple orchards thrive along the southern shore of Georgian Bay and the northern shores of Lake Erie and Lake Ontario.

Farming depends heavily on current market trends. As people eat less red meat, fewer farmers raise beef cattle. Former tobacco farms are now producing other crops as people learn more about the dangers of smoking. The number of crop farms has increased lately, but this trend may change if customer demand changes.

Mining

During the 1870s, one of the Ontario government's main concerns was to open up new territories and develop its industries. It therefore encouraged mining by making it very easy for prospectors to stake and register a claim. The fee for a prospector's licence was small, and mineral rights to land cost only $2.50 a hectare (a dollar an acre). The discovery of the vast nickel deposits around Sudbury in 1883 made the Mowat administration rethink its policy. Potential revenues from the new mines were enormous — surely some

Left: **Slag drains from INCO's smelter at Sudbury.** *Above*: **The Hemlo gold mine**

could be spared for a growing government badly in need of funds. Licence fees were raised and a tax was imposed on minerals extracted from the ground. The mining companies complained, but they paid.

In the early 1900s, as the railways penetrated deeper into the northern hinterland, there were several gold and silver rushes on towns such as Cobalt, Kirkland Lake and Porcupine. During the Great Depression, gold mining boomed in northern Ontario, creating fortunes for speculators, such as E.P. Taylor. The Second World War stimulated the mining industry. An iron ore mine was sunk at Steep Rock, and older mines stepped up production to provide the raw materials for motor vehicles, ships, guns, shells and aircraft.

Gold was once the most important mineral mined in northern Ontario, but as the ore grew scarcer and therefore more costly to recover, production went into a steady decline. Although Timmins, Kirkland Lake and Red Lake still produce some gold, they have had to branch out into other types of industry. The Hemlo Gold Mines have recently revived interest in mining gold.

Nickel and copper are now the two main minerals produced in Ontario. Sudbury produces a fifth of the world's nickel. Zinc is Ontario's third most valuable mineral. It is mined at Timmins and other northern sites.

Forestry

The Crown owns almost all of Ontario's productive forest land. In practice, this means that the Ontario government sells licences to private companies to harvest areas of forest.

In the 1820s squared white pine logs sold to the British and Americans made up 50 percent of Canada's exports. By the 1840s, lumbering (the sawing of trees into planks) was a major industry and many communities had a sawmill powered by a nearby stream. The largest of Ontario's early mills was run by the Egan Company in the Ottawa Valley. During the winter of 1855, this one company had 3800 men cutting trees in the woods.

Ontario's pulp and paper industry began in 1887, when a mill at Cornwall produced the first paper made in the province. It was not until 1913, when the United States dropped all tariffs against Canadian pulp and paper, that mills were built in other locations, including Thorold, Trenton and Sault Ste. Marie. Today there are about twenty pulp and paper mills in Ontario, mostly in the north.

Right: The James Bay Pulp Mill at Marathon.
Far right: The Algoma Steel plant at Sault Ste Marie, the country's second-biggest (after Hamilton) steel-producing centre

These mills are close to major rivers and to large bodies of water such as Lakes Huron, Superior and Nipissing.

Furniture grades of veneer (a thin layer of wood made from hardwood trees) are manufactured in Sault Ste. Marie and Thessalon. Plywood is made from poplar in Cochrane and Hearst. Mills at New Liskeard, Kirkland Lake and Sturgeon Falls make particle board. The number of sawmills in Ontario is steadily declining. This is a result of several factors — public reaction to pollution, the higher cost of power and the aging of machinery.

Steelmaking

Steelmaking has been a leading industry in Ontario for a long time. Most of the province's steelmaking takes place in Hamilton, on the western shore of Lake Ontario, and in Sault Ste. Marie at the head of Lake Huron. Hamilton is a good location for steelmaking because it is close to Ontario's industrial centre which needs steel for manufacturing. Large rolling and fabricating mills that produce sheets of steel are located along the north shore of Lake Ontario.

Cars

The automobile industry began in Ontario in 1904, when the Ford Motor Company opened a plant in Windsor, near its major Detroit operations. In 1907, Sam McLaughlin, the son of an Oshawa carriage-maker, set up the McLaughlin Motor Car Company, the forerunner of General Motors of Canada, in Oshawa. Automobile plants dotted around the edges of Toronto now provide work for many thousands of Ontarians. In recent years two leading Japanese car manufacturers have built assembly plants in Ontario — Toyota in Cambridge and Honda in Alliston.

Most of the plants involved in Ontario's automobile industry make parts that are assembled elsewhere, for manufacturers find that specialized plants operate most efficiently. Almost a quarter of all the industry in Ontario relates to automobiles.

CHAPTER 7

Environmental Concerns

Ontario is Canada's most heavily industrialized province, and its people are concerned about the quality of its water, air and soil. Their concern is not entirely new. In 1832, when Toronto was still York, a writer complained of the state of its harbour in winter: "All the filth of the town — dead horses, dogs, cats, manure, etc. heaped up together on the ice, to drop down in a few days into the water... If they have no regard for the health of their fellow-beings, are they not afraid to poison the fish that supply their own tables?"

That particular problem was solved — for the time being — by the installation of sewage systems and garbage collection. But it soon resurfaced in other forms and other places as the population of Ontario grew and its industries multiplied.

Back in 1832, and indeed as recently as thirty years ago, people thought that pollution could only be felt, smelled or seen. Itchy eyes, sore throats and foul-smelling water with floating garbage were the only recognized evidence of pollution. Now people know that pollution may be invisible and odourless. In 1957, the Ontario Water Resources Commission began to tackle the widespread problem of water quality. Since then the clean-up of Ontario's lakes, air and soil has been extensive, but it has also been expensive and slow. As efforts continue, greater stress is being placed on education and research in hopes of preventing further increases in levels of pollution.

Moose family in northern Ontario. During recent years Ontarians have become more and more concerned about environmental issues such as air and water pollution and the destruction of wildlife habitat.

Water Pollution

What happened to the English-Wabigoon river system provides a painful example of invisible pollution. In 1970, it was discovered that people of the Grassy Narrows Reserve on that river system were slowly being poisoned by mercury in the fish they caught and ate. The mercury was in waste material that had been dumped into the river for years by a nearby paper mill. The result for the natives of Grassy Narrows was devastating: their jobs as commercial fishermen were gone; their main food resource was denied them; and the health of many was very seriously damaged. It is thought that it will be a hundred years or more before the water and fish of the English-Wabigoon system are again safe to drink and eat.

Another cause of serious water pollution in Ontario is toxic chemicals. The industries surrounding the Great Lakes use over 60 000 different chemicals. Ontario hospitals use more than 15 000 different drugs, and producers mix over 1500 flavours and additives into the foods that Ontarians eat. All of these chemicals would

Tom Thomson Island, Algonquin Park

find their way into Lakes Ontario and Erie if the province did not treat its sewage. This practice began in earnest in the 1960s, when Lake Erie became so polluted that its water was clogged with algae. The algae killed the lake's wildlife and in doing so, damaged two important industries: fishing and tourism. Intensive clean-up efforts and legislation have helped to reverse the damage done to the lake.

Yet another cause of water pollution is acid rain. Most of the acid rain that falls into Ontario's lakes originates far away in the industrial heartland of the northeastern United States. Programs undertaken jointly by American and Canadian governments have been set up to reduce acid rain emissions from industrial smokestacks in both countries. Acid rain levels are measured and tracked at Dorset, a village in Ontario's cottage country, one of the regions most sensitive to this type of pollution. Acid rain threatens the life of the province's forests as well as that of its lakes and many people consider it one of Ontario's most serious environmental problems.

There are several other causes of water pollution as well. Bacteria from untreated human sewage that has been dumped into lakes is one source of pollution that can be removed by water-treatment plants. Most communities in Ontario now have water-treatment facilities funded by all three levels of government. Three other causes of water pollution — organic waste, excessive nutrients and hot water emissions — come from industrial uses of water and are now controlled by legislation.

Ontario's sparkling lakes and flowing rivers have six main uses: drinking water, transportation, fishing, recreation, generating power and manufacturing processes. All of these contribute to the high standard of living that Ontarians enjoy. For these reasons, it is vital to protect this magnificent resource.

Air Pollution

Most of the air pollution in Ontario is caused by the burning of fossil fuels such as oil, coal and gas. Much of the time it is hardly noticeable, though it can still have a damaging effect on plants and buildings. Sometimes, however, weather conditions keep the noxious emissions from cars and industries from dispersing. The resulting fumes create a smog that irritates eyes and breathing passages, and that can even be life-threatening to people with respiratory problems. In recent years, legislation aimed at reducing air pollution has required industries to install filters on smokestacks, remove lead from gasoline and design better exhaust systems for cars.

A reforested area planted with red pines. *Inset*: A logging truck in Algonquin Park. Logging is strictly controlled in the park, but many people feel it should not be allowed at all.

**Cars on Toronto's
Don Valley
Parkway**

Soil Pollution

Soil pollution has several causes, not least of which is careless waste disposal. In one case, thousands of tonnes of slightly radioactive waste were dumped some years ago around the town of Port Hope, a uranium refining centre about 60 kilometres (37 miles) east of Toronto. Later, when the town grew, the material had to be removed from under houses and other buildings, including schools, to reduce the risk of cancer for local residents.

Sometimes soil is polluted by a contaminant in the air that settles on the ground. The children in Toronto's Riverdale district, for instance, are periodically tested for levels of lead in their blood. The tests are necessary because these children play in the sand and earth of playgrounds that were in the path of smoke from factories and incinerators along Toronto's lakeshore.

One solution to the airborne pollutants that might settle and contaminate soil is to build taller industrial smokestacks, so that wind

Top: INCO's superstack at Sudbury. *Above*: In February 1990, a dump containing 14 million tires caught fire in the town of Hagersville. It took firefighters 17 days to put out the fire, and a year and a half later the clean-up was still not completed. *Right*: The weekly garbage pickup of recyclable items has been a big success in Metropolitan Toronto and many other Ontario municipalities.

can carry and dilute the pollution over a larger area. The INCO factory in Sudbury took this step after it became clear that the wildlife in the region was dying. The result has been good locally: the wildlife is recovering. But the smokestack has been pinpointed as one of Canada's main causes of acid rain over a much larger region.

Some soil pollution is caused by household and industrial garbage. The message that 50 percent of household garbage is recyclable has gotten through to governments, and most Ontario communities now participate in residential recycling programs. Industrial garbage is often broken down so that reusable chemicals can be removed and repackaged, and non-usable chemicals can be filtered into solid waste and disposed of in special sites.

Government Action

The Ontario government has always responded quickly to environmental issues as they arise. In 1971, Ontario banned the use of the chemical DDT in pesticides because this substance was found to damage birds that ate insects exposed to it. The 1979 toxic leak from a train derailment in Mississauga led to the passing of a law that controlled the transport of dangerous goods. Under this law, all hazardous goods must be labelled and traceable at every stage of their journey. Violators of this law can be fined up to $100 000.

Passing laws against pollution is often difficult. Industries sometimes argue that the costs of clean-up measures would be crippling and they would have to close down, throwing hundreds of employees out of work. Some situations involve different levels of government and often the governments of other countries as well. Chemicals from Japan are found in the snow of northern Ontario. Sulphur dioxide from the American state of Ohio falls as acid rain in Ontario's cottage country. Chemicals from Sudbury's smokestacks fall on Quebec's lakes. It takes time for local, provincial, federal and foreign governments to work out solutions to the global problems of pollution.

CHAPTER 8

Government

The Government of Ontario is democratic — that is, it is run by officials who are elected by the people to represent their views. Provincial elections are generally held every four years, and any Canadian citizen who is eighteen years of age or over and lives in Ontario may vote in these elections.

The premier of the province is the leader of the political party that wins the most seats in the election. The three main political parties in Ontario are the Liberal Party, the New Democratic Party and the Progressive Conservative Party.

The people of Ontario have — or at least had — a history of remaining loyal to a political party for a long time. The Liberal Party, for example, governed Ontario from 1871 to 1905; for all but fifteen years or so after that, Progressive Conservatives were in power — until 1985. In that year, the Liberals formed a minority government, and two years later, they were returned with an overwhelming majority. But when they called an election in 1990, victory went to the New Democrats, who in turn gave way to the Conservatives in 1995. It remains to be seen whether these recent turn-arounds signal an enduring change in the behaviour of Ontario voters.

Revenue

The Government of Ontario uses several methods of raising funds to carry out its many functions, including a variety of taxes.

The impressive Provincial Parliament Building stands amid the lawns and flowerbeds of Queen's Park in the heart of Toronto.

Retailers collect a sales tax on most goods Ontarians buy and transmit this tax to the provincial government. Food, books and a few other items are exempt. Income tax is charged on the money that provincial residents earn. The percent of their income that individuals pay in income tax varies with the amount they earn. People who make significantly more money than the average earner may pay almost half their income to different levels of government. There are also taxes imposed on businesses and special taxes on liquor, cigarettes and gasoline.

Licence and permit fees and payments related to natural resources also provide government revenue.

In return for paying taxes and fees, the citizens of Ontario enjoy one of the highest standards of living in the world. Their hospitals are modern and well run, their transportation systems are efficient and extensive, and their education system is available to all residents.

Medical Care

In 1945, the Government of Canada proposed a national health system as part of its social programs package. Ontario rejected the notion of medicare, and it was not until 1967 that a full health insurance plan was established in the province.

The government of Ontario now funds about 200 general and 40 special hospitals. It pays about 18 000 doctors for their services and 60 000 nurses for their professional care. In addition, the government has about 100 000 salaried health-support workers on its payroll. This medical system is paid for through taxes and federal transfer payments.

Roads

Upper Canada's roads were mainly mud tracks that disappeared whenever it rained and were dusty and full of potholes and tree

Chatham, 1838, and a typical road of the times

stumps at the best of times. In some places there were narrow "corduroy" roads with a surface made of cedar logs laid side by side at right angles to the road's direction. Wagons lurched over the logs, carrying settlers and their goods deeper into the interior of the province. Military units built the main roads — Yonge Street, running from York (now Toronto) to Lake Simcoe; Dundas Road from York to the Thames River, where London is now located; and the Kingston Road linking York and Kingston. Settlers were supposed to put several days' work a year into building roads, but not many actually did.

Today thousands of kilometres of paved and unpaved roads link Ontario's villages, towns and cities. The maintenance of these roads is the responsibility of provincial and local (municipal) governments. Governments are also responsible for building new roads to keep pace with a growing population.

The super highway system across southern Ontario provides an excellent transportation route between Montreal and Windsor. GO

Top: An interchange on Highway 401, which crosses the northern end of Toronto. *Above*: The GO Transit system of commuter trains and buses carries about 120 000 passengers a day on its seven routes.

Transit, a publicly run rail and road network, serves commuters along the north shore of Lake Ontario from Hamilton to Oshawa and north to Barrie. The Trans-Canada Highway, a joint federal-provincial responsibility, runs across the province from Ottawa, along the north shore of Lake Superior, to the Manitoba border.

Left: **University College and Hart House on the University of Toronto's main campus in downtown Toronto.** *Above*: **Lakehead University at Thunder Bay**

Education

A government-financed public school system began in 1841, in the mostly Protestant region of Upper Canada. Its standards were set by Egerton Ryerson, a Methodist minister who was chief superintendent of education from 1844 to 1876. Ryerson believed that education should be free and compulsory for all children, and that publicly financed schools should teach Christian moral values as well as academic subjects but not be connected with any specific religious denomination, or group.

Today, Ontario has a dual publicly financed school system that includes "public" non-denominational schools and "separate" Roman Catholic schools.

School boards composed of elected representatives from the community have the responsibility of running both types of elementary and secondary schools. These boards are allowed to raise money for their schools by means of property taxes with taxpayers directing their tax dollars to either the public or separate system as they choose.

There are three levels of education in Ontario. Each year, the elementary and secondary levels educate almost two million children, and the post-secondary level educates over 350 000 students in almost fifty colleges and universities.

Provincial Parks

The Government of Ontario owns and manages over 250 parks, including eight wilderness parks that cover over four million hectares (15 000 square miles) of land. Natural environment parks and smaller nature reserve parks cover over a million hectares (4000 square miles) more. The government protects the natural beauty of

Two of Ontario's eight wilderness parks — Killarney Provincial Park on the north shore of Georgian Bay and (*inset*) Quetico Provincial Park, west of Lake Superior

these parks from commercial or residential development. Smaller parks dotted about the province include historic sites and recreational parks.

The popularity of Ontario's parks is shown by the number of visitors that they attract every year. Seven million people, including many Ontarians, enjoy the natural beauty and recreation facilities of Ontario's rich park network.

Federal Representation

In federal elections, Ontarians elect ninety-nine Members of Parliament to represent their concerns in the House of Commons. The province also has twenty-four Senate seats.

Left: **Toronto's much-admired City Hall was completed in 1965.**
Above: **The Stratford City Hall**

CHAPTER 9

Culture and Sports

The fact that Ontario has produced many outstanding artists, performers, writers and athletes should come as no surprise. The province does, after all, have almost one-third of the country's population.

Not that all the talent on display is home-grown. Toronto is the centre of the English-language publishing, movie, TV and recording industries, and it is home to some of the country's foremost cultural institutions, including the Royal Conservatory of Music, the Ontario College of Art and the National Ballet School. As such, it attracts talented people from across the country and from abroad. Well-known "imports" include novelists Josef Skvorecky and Austin Clarke; guitarist Liona Boyd, pianist Anton Kuerti, and sculptor Sorel Etrog — not to mention almost the entire Toronto Blue Jays team.

Of course, Ontario exports talent as well. Ontarians who left to seek fame and fortune in New York, London and Hollywood include Mary Pickford, Beatrice Lillie, Raymond Massey, Hume Cronyn, Paul Anka and Neil Young.

Art

Many talented and influential artists have come from Ontario. The most famous, without doubt, are Tom Thomson, who died mysteriously in 1917, and several of the seven painters who began exhibiting together in Toronto in 1920 as the Group of Seven. With

Overleaf: **The National Ballet Company in a performance of *Csardas***

Both *Artist's Wife and Daughter*, by
Norval Morrisseau, and Tom Thomson's
Afternoon, Algonquin Park, are at the
McMichael Gallery in Kleinburg.
Salmon Run, a sculpture by Susan
Schelle, can be seen near Toronto's
SkyDome.

broad decisive strokes, these artists captured the stark beauty of the
land they painted — the Canadian Shield. Their fresh approach
coloured the way a whole generation of artists interpreted Canada's
landscape. Much of the work of the Group of Seven is now housed
in the McMichael Gallery in Kleinburg, just north of Toronto. More
recently, Norval Morrisseau, who grew up on a reserve near Lake
Nipigon, began painting to record Ojibwa legends. Ken Danby has
painted hundreds of athletes in action. As well as drawing and
painting, Michael Snow works in several media, including sculpture, photography and film. So did Harold Town, who was perhaps
the most versatile artist Canada has yet produced.

The National Gallery of Canada, Ottawa. This spectacular glass and granite building designed by Israeli-born architect Moshe Safdie is a fitting home for the gallery's collection of over 40 000 works of art.

The National Gallery in Ottawa has been supporting Canadian artists since it was founded in 1890. With funding from the federal government, the Gallery commissions and collects works by Canadian painters and sculptors. These and the gallery's smaller collections of European and American art are now housed in a cathedral-like building, much of which is made of glass.

Not all of Ontario's art is enclosed in galleries. The monumental aluminum and steel sculptures of Kosso Eloul adorn city spaces, outside the province as well as within it. Michael Snow's flock of geese soars above the heads of shoppers in Toronto's Eaton Centre. Indian rock paintings are found throughout the province at sites including Missinaibi Lake, which lies north of Lake Superior, and Mazinaw Lake north of Napanee. The largest collection of these paintings is probably north of Peterborough.

Literature

Ontarians have long excelled in every kind of writing. Poet and entertainer Pauline Johnson was an international celebrity at the turn of the century; novelist Sara Jeanette Duncan's works are enjoying something of a revival after half a century of neglect; Stephen Leacock, whose *Sunshine Sketches of a Little Town* was published in 1912, remains the country's unsurpassed master of humour.

More recent award-winning Ontario writers include novelists Timothy Findley, Marian Engel and Morley Callaghan; poets James Reaney and Al Purdy; short-story writer Alice Munro; historians Donald Creighton and J.M.S. Careless; children's writers Jean Little, Janet Lunn, Bernice Thurman Hunter and wildly popular storyteller, Robert Munsch.

Several writers are as remarkable for their versatility as for the quality of their work. Dennis Lee wrote highly acclaimed poetry for adults before he began delighting children with *Alligator Pie*, and he continues to write successfully for both audiences. Margaret Atwood won her first Governor General's Award in 1966 for her book of poems *The Circle Game* and her second in 1985 for her novel *The Handmaid's Tale*; she has also published highly praised works of literary criticism and short stories.

Robertson Davies was a successful playwright, newspaper columnist and winner of the Leacock Medal for humour well before his novels of the seventies and eighties won him the international acclaim he enjoys today. Pierre Berton is widely known as a writer of popular history, social critic, TV personality and newspaper columnist. Michael Ondaatje writes poetry and prose, fiction and non-fiction and makes films as well.

The lists could go on.

Music

Talented Ontario musicians have contributed greatly to all aspects of the North American musical scene. The trio Sharon, Lois and

Left: Bruce Cockburn in concert at Ontario Place. *Above*: A father/son performance at the Mariposa Folk Festival

Bram enthrall child audiences all over the province and beyond. Paul Anka recorded "Diana" at the age of 15, and became an international celebrity almost overnight. Folk singer and song writer Gordon Lightfoot has won wide acclaim across the continent. Glenn Gould, born in Toronto, was perhaps Canada's finest pianist, and left behind a legacy of over eighty highly praised recordings of classical music. Two of Canada's internationally admired opera singers — Maureen Forrester and Teresa Stratas — live in Ontario as do two of the country's most successful composers Harry Somers and R. Murray Schafer. Albums by Alannah Myles, Bruce Cockburn and Shania Twain have sold in the hundreds of thousands.

Excellent symphony orchestras are based in Ottawa, Thunder Bay and Sudbury, and Toronto is home to several groups,

Left: **A performance by Opera Hamilton of** *La Traviata.*
Above: **Musicians of the Toronto Symphony Orchestra under the direction of Jukka-Pekka Saraste, conductor.**

both classical and popular, that have world-wide reputations. These include the Canadian Opera Company, the Toronto Symphony Orchestra, the Toronto Mendelssohn Choir and rock groups Rush and Blue Rodeo.

Much of Ontario's popular music can be enjoyed by audiences out of doors. Ontario Place, on Toronto's waterfront, is an amusement park that includes a large outdoor amphitheatre where symphonies and rock groups perform in the summer. Toronto and Ottawa both have summer lunch-time concerts in downtown open-air venues, and several Muskoka towns feature concerts by their water's edge on summer evenings. The Mariposa Festival is a popular folk music event that has been held outdoors in various locations for over thirty years.

Dance

Canada's National Ballet Company based in Toronto, has an international reputation for excellence and performs in countries around the world. Children from across Canada audition for a place in the National Ballet School, the training ground for Canada's ballet dancers. British-born Celia Franca was the driving force behind the company in its early years, and Betty Oliphant was the first principal of the school. Among the National's many outstanding principal dancers, past and present, are Karen Kain, Frank Augustyn, Veronica Tennant, Yoko Ichino, Kevin Pugh, Gregory Osborne and Margaret Illman.

In addition to the National Ballet, Ontario has a number of smaller dance troupes based in Toronto and elsewhere. Seen here are (*left*) the innovative and widely acclaimed Desrosiers Dance Theatre and (*right*) the Canadian Children's Dance Theatre, a modern troupe of 16 dancers aged 8 to 18.

Theatre

Ontario's theatre companies perform for audiences across the province, sometimes on mobile platforms in high school gymnasiums, sometimes outdoors in parks, sometimes at festivals that have become major tourist attractions. The Stratford Festival transforms that small town into a major theatre centre every summer. Guest directors and actors join some of Canada's finest performers to present plays by Shakespeare and other famous playwrights. Guelph's Spring Festival presents musicians, plays, films and art showings. In May, the Shaw Festival at Niagara-on-the-Lake begins its season of performances.

While there are large or small theatre groups in many places, including Sudbury, Hamilton and Ottawa, Toronto, with about 130 companies performing on forty-five stages, is obviously the main centre of theatrical activities in Ontario. It has been said that you could spend a year and see a different live performance every night. The stages range from gilt and plush elegance to converted warehouses, and the productions from elaborate musicals and the classics to the newest experimental Canadian plays. Several companies perform outdoors in the summer.

The Stratford Festival's production of the Rodgers and Hammerstein musical *Carousel*

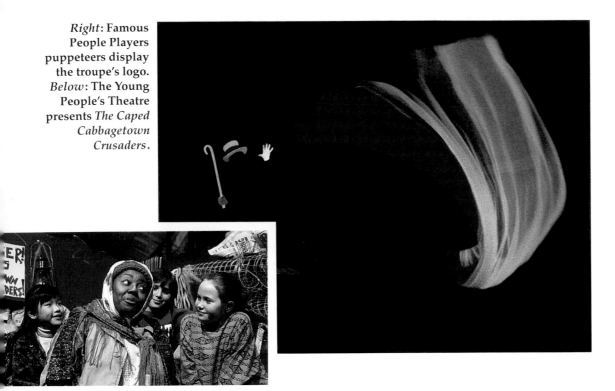

Right: Famous People Players puppeteers display the troupe's logo. *Below*: The Young People's Theatre presents *The Caped Cabbagetown Crusaders*.

Of the many companies, two deserve special mention for their uniqueness and durability. The Toronto Young People's Theatre was founded in 1965 by Susan Rubes. Today it is the largest producing theatre for young people in North America, presenting fourteen attractions a year in its two theatres. It also runs a theatre-school year-round and a touring program. The Famous People Players, founded by Diane Duprey in 1974, is a troupe composed mainly of mentally handicapped young adults. Their blacklight puppet shows tour widely through North America — and occasionally as far afield as China — always to great acclaim.

Not all of Ontario's theatre companies perform in English. There are well-established francophone companies in Toronto (Théâtre Français), Ottawa (Théâtre français du Centre national des Arts)

Left: Comedians Johnny Wayne and Frank Shuster in a CBC TV spoof of *Macbeth*. *Right*: From 1987 through 1990, the *Degrassi Junior High* and *Degrassi High* series collected dozens of awards and fans in 40 countries.

and Sudbury (Théâtre du Nouvel-Ontario). In Toronto there are also regular productions in Hungarian, Italian and other languages.

Many Ontario actors have achieved international fame, including Christopher Plummer, Kate Reid, Kate Nelligan, Al Waxman — and probably the most famous of them all, Lorne Greene. Known to an older generation as "The Voice of Doom," Greene read the network news during the early days of the Second World War. He later appeared on Broadway, at Stratford and in a few minor movies, but is most widely remembered as *Bonanza's* Ben Cartwright, a TV role he played for fourteen years. Film directors who have made their mark on the international scene include Norman Jewison, whose film *In the Heat of the Night* won the Academy Award for best picture in 1967, David Cronenberg and Atom Egoyan.

Festivals

Several yearly festivals reflect the ethnic origins of Ontario's communities. Oktoberfests in Kitchener-Waterloo and London mark the German community's celebration of harvest with beer halls and oompah bands. The Bon Soo Winter Carnival held in Sault Ste. Marie celebrates the North with its dog-sled races. The Miner's Festival in Cobalt includes French-Canadian step dancing and a canoe marathon. Caravan, a nine-day multicultural festival held in Toronto each June transforms more than forty halls, gymnasiums and other sites around the city into "pavilions" that showcase the crafts, dances, songs and foods of the city's many cultures. Caribana, in early August is the West Indian community's chance to celebrate its roots. The Six Nations' Pageant is held in a forest amphitheatre on August weekends at the Brantford Reserve, and pow-wows are held in Sarnia, Sioux Narrows, Blind River and several other places.

Below: A spectacular parade is the highlight of Caribana, the Toronto West Indian community's 10-day celebration of its culture. *Right*: The Dragon Dance is an important part of Chinese New Year festivities.

94

Sports

The people of Ontario are active in a wide variety of sports all year round. In winter, downhill skiing, cross-country skiing, skating and tobogganing are all family activities to be enjoyed in Ontario's vast network of parks and privately owned resorts. In summer, Ontarians take to the lakes, woods and roads to swim, sail, canoe, hike, jog and cycle.

Left: Cyclists enjoy the pleasant paths set aside for them in Toronto. *Lower left*: Windsurfing on Georgian Bay. *Below*: Ottawa's annual National Capital Marathon

At Toronto's SkyDome, seating capacity for baseball games is 50 600. Loyal Blue Jay fans turn out in such numbers that they have been setting American League attendance records since 1990. Their devotion was rewarded in 1992 and 1993 when the Jays won the World Series back to back.

The province has been producing athletic champions for more than a century. In 1880, Toronto oarsman Ned Hanlan became a national hero as the first Canadian to win a world championship. Ontario's men and women continued this rowing tradition at the 1996 Summer Olympics Games winning gold in the women's double sculls, silver in the women's eights, men's single sculls and men's lightweight fours, and bronze in the women's quad sculls.

Tom Longboat, from the Six Nations Reserve, won the Boston Marathon in 1907 and for several years afterwards was considered the best long-distance runner in America. At the 1996 Summer Olympics, reigning world champion Donovan Bailey from Oakville won a gold medal, in world-record-breaking time, in the 100-metre dash and a second gold as anchor to the men's 4×100-metre relay race.

Many Ontario skiers and skaters have won international fame. Anne Heggtveit of Ottawa won Canada's first Olympic gold medal for skiing in 1960. Steve Podborski of Toronto was the first North American to win the men's World Cup downhill skiing championship in 1982.

Far left: Barbara Ann Scott was the first Canadian figure skater to win an Olympic Gold Medal. *Left*: Elizabeth Manley, Silver Medallist at the 1988 Calgary Olympics

Hockey greats Bobby Hull, Bobby Orr and Phil Esposito were born and grew up in Ontario. Wayne Gretzky, widely nicknamed "The Great One", learned to play on a backyard rink in Brantford. The list of Ontario's medal-winning figure skaters includes Barbara Ann Scott, Otto and Maria Jelinek, Brian Orser, Elizabeth Manley, Toller Cranston and Elvis Stojko.

Many of Canada's finest swimmers live in Ontario. Alex Bauman came to Canada when he was five, and by the time he reached seventeen, he was hailed as the world's fastest swimmer. In 1981, he set four new Canadian records and a new world record, and by 1983 he had won many gold medals. George Young and Marilyn Bell are two of Ontario's famous long-distance swimmers. In 1927, Young became known as the "Catalina Kid" because he swam the Catalina Channel in less than sixteen hours, winning against a hundred champions. Marilyn Bell was the first person to swim across Lake Ontario and the youngest person ever to swim the English Channel.

A new milestone in Canadian sports history was attained in 1991 when Ferguson Jenkins of Chatham, Ontario, became the first Canadian inducted into the Baseball Hall of Fame.

CHAPTER 10
Around the Province

Opposite Page: Grain terminal, Thunder Bay. *Inset*: Cricket match at Sunnybrook Park (top); oil refinery, Sarnia (bottom). *Above, clockwise from top left*: Don Valley, Toronto; scarecrow in a southern Ontario cornfield; piper, Old Fort William; orcas at Marineland, Niagara-on-the-Lake

Toronto's history as a community goes back almost two centuries to the founding of the Town of York, in 1793, by John Graves Simcoe, the first lieutenant-governor of Upper Canada. During the War of 1812, Americans captured Fort York and burnt the legislature. Canadians rebuilt the town after the war and settled the surrounding lands. York grew rapidly and became a centre of commercial and industrial activity. As it grew and changed, it earned various nicknames: first "Muddy York," then "Hogtown," and sometime after being renamed, "Toronto the Good." Now, with a population of about three million, Toronto is the largest city in Canada and is known as the financial capital of the country. It has vibrant ethnic communities, a wide range of cultural and sporting activities, a dramatic waterfront skyline and old, tree-lined streets.

The dynamic modern architecture of the past few decades reflects the evolution of Toronto from a staid, conservative city to an exciting world-class centre. The CN Tower is the world's tallest free-standing structure, offering a point of reference that is visible for miles. The curved twin towers of Toronto's City Hall cradle Nathan Phillips Square, a centre of ethnic festivals, free art exhibits, skating in winter and lively concerts by local musicians in summer. The SkyDome, a sports arena in downtown Toronto, has a retractable roof that allows the local American League baseball team, the Blue Jays, to play ball, rain or shine. The Eaton Centre, with its soaring glass walls and open areas is a popular place to meet as well as to shop. The modern O'Keefe Centre and several graciously renovated smaller theatres — St. Lawrence Centre for the Arts, the Royal Alexandra, the Pantages — are just a few of Toronto's theatres.

Toronto scenes, *clockwise from bottom*: Skyline from the lake; the Leslie Street Spit, home to North America's biggest nesting colony of ring-billed gulls; the Eaton Centre, with artist Michael Snow's flock of Canada geese; the Art Gallery of Ontario

Above: Casa Loma, the fairytale castle built by industrialist Sir Henry Pellatt. *Top Right*: Ontario Place, an indoor-outdoor entertainment centre built on three artificial islands. *Bottom*: Dinosaur exhibit at the Royal Ontario Museum

Roy Thomson Hall is a dome-shaped concert hall that provides a stage for the best Canadian and international musicians. The 287-hectare (710-acre) Metro Toronto Zoo, with over 4000 animals, is known world-wide for its innovative design, which integrates structures, land use and the landscape.

Toronto also has world-class museums and art galleries. The many and varied treasures housed in the Royal Ontario Museum include one of the best Chinese collections to be found anywhere outside of China and an excellent Egyptian collection, with displays of mummies, models and jewellery. One of the province's most popular spots to visit is the Ontario Science Centre, situated in a modern building that wanders down the sides of a deep ravine. The Centre has over 800 hands-on exhibits, and visitors can operate

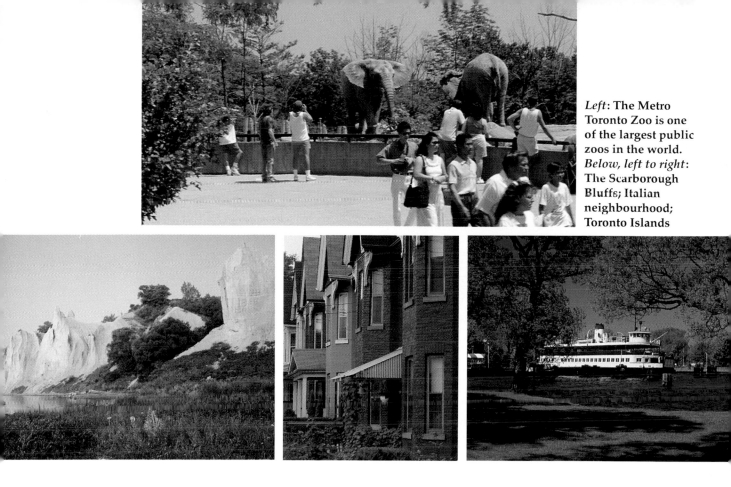

Left: The Metro Toronto Zoo is one of the largest public zoos in the world. *Below, left to right*: The Scarborough Bluffs; Italian neighbourhood; Toronto Islands

pumps, microscopes, musical instruments and radios, and be subjected to static electricity that makes their hair stand on end.

The Art Gallery of Ontario, also located in Toronto, contains the largest collection in the world of Henry Moore's sculptures and sketches. Also displayed are works by world-famous artists such as Rodin, Renoir, Tintoretto and Augustus John.

The setting of Toronto is one of great natural beauty. The city is criss-crossed by ravines and rivers, the basis of a network of trails and parks. The city also has sand beaches, white cliffs and a windswept group of islands a short ferry trip away. High Park has over 150 hectares (400 acres) of woods and fields, and a large pond that attracts many water birds. Edwards Gardens, in Toronto's Don Mills area, is a gardener's delight.

The Golden Horseshoe

The Golden Horseshoe is the densely populated and highly industrialized area that stretches around the western shore of Lake Ontario. It is an area rich in history, culture, business and industry. On these shores, French, English, Americans and natives battled one another over centuries. Here are world-famous natural and historic sites, museums, galleries, concert halls, theatres and splendid buildings old and new. Car plants in Oshawa and Oakville, steel manufacturing in Hamilton, wine-making in and around St. Catharines and the tourist industry in Niagara Falls, are all vital to the economy of Canada.

Above: Hamilton's Royal Botanical Gardens, a 1000-ha (2700-acre) park that includes many delightful flower displays and a wildlife sanctuary. *Right*: The Clock Tower at Niagara-on-the-Lake. The town, originally named Newark, was the province's capital until 1796.

Southwestern Ontario

Southwestern Ontario has fertile farmland and many pretty towns and small cities that are rich in history, beauty, theatre and rural traditions. The most southern point in Ontario is Point Pelee National Park, a 1600-hectare (4000-acre) sanctuary for birds and, in September, for migrating Monarch butterflies. Canada's most southern city is Windsor, which has many car-manufacturing plants. The Reverend Josiah Henson, a slave who escaped to freedom in Canada, lived in Dresden, near Chatham. Many people think that Harriet Beecher Stowe, the famous author of *Uncle Tom's Cabin* based her novel on Josiah Henson's life. His house is part of Uncle Tom's Cabin Museum.

London, site of the University of Western Ontario, Sir Adam Beck's home, a pioneer brewery and Ontario's oldest fall fair, was

Left: The fort-like London Courthouse is said to have been modelled on Colonel Thomas Talbot's ancestral home in Ireland. *Below*: People come from far and wide to shop at the Kitchener-Waterloo farmers' markets.

once considered a possible capital of Ontario. Brantford, on the Grand River, is named for Chief Joseph Brant, who brought his Loyalist Mohawks here in 1784. The town is also known for the invention of the telephone by Alexander Graham Bell. Goderich has the largest harbour on the east side of Lake Huron and huge waterfront grain elevators.

In the centre of southwestern Ontario lies Stratford, a pleasant old town which, every summer, hosts some of the finest Shakespearean drama performed in North America. Nearby is Kitchener-Waterloo, the market community of the surrounding Amish and Mennonite farming families.

Left: The Stratford Theatre. *Below*: The boardwalk across the Point Pelee marsh pond. *Lower Right*: A friendly giraffe at the African Lion Safari and Game Farm

Georgian Bay

From Tobermory, a tiny village at the tip of the Bruce Peninsula, to Midland on the east shore, the clear, cold waters of Georgian Bay wash against long sand beaches and rocky shores. The limestone spit that forms the Bruce Peninsula is the northern extension of the Niagara Escarpment, and hikers along the almost 700-kilometre (435-mile) Bruce Trail enjoy superb views of the bay from 100-metre (300-foot) high vantage points. Collingwood, with its ski hills, Wasaga Beach, with its white sands, and Midland and Penetanguishene with their historic traditions, all make this part of Ontario a beautiful place to live, play and work.

Below: Pointe-au-Baril Lighthouse on Georgian Bay. *Left*: The *Martyrs' Shrine* at Midland commemorates the six Jesuit missionaries who were killed at Sainte-Marie.

Blue Mountain, at Collingwood, is one of Ontario's most popular ski areas. *Inset*: Wasaga Beach

Eastern Ontario

Upper Canada Village, near Morrisburg, is a reconstruction of houses, churches and businesses of the late 1700s and 1800s. Re-enactments of pioneer life allow visitors to watch oxen plowing the fields, blacksmiths and printers turning out their wares, women spinning, weaving and cooking, a teacher and students going through their lessons in a log school. On view in the school — but unused — are a leather strap and a birch rod for punishing students who misbehaved.

Kingston, on the north shore of Lake Ontario, has been a Native village, a French fort and trading post, a British fort, and even for a short while, the capital of the United Province of Canada. Today it

Far Left: The Fort Henry Guard. *Left*: Pioneer life is re-enacted at Upper Canada Village, Morrisburg. *Below*: Sandbanks Provincial Park in Prince Edward County

is a prosperous and attractive city with many fine old limestone buildings. Belleville, between Kingston and Toronto, overlooks the Bay of Quinte. The Hastings County Museum there has a wonderful collection of lighting devices, such as soapstone lamps, candles from ancient Rome and torches.

The Prince Edward County Peninsula, with its lovely pastoral countryside, was settled by Loyalist refugees from the American War of Independence. Their influence is recorded in the Loyalist Museum at Adolphustown. The peninsula is known for its sweeping dunes near Picton, its lush golf courses and its fine swimming.

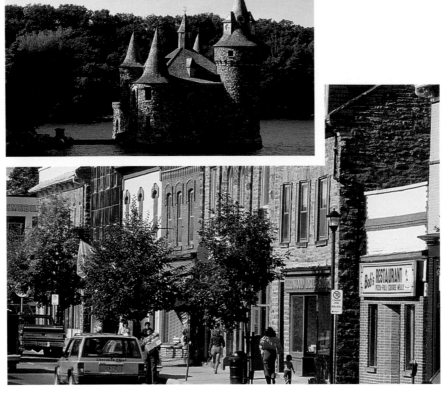

Top: Boldt Castle. American millionaire George Boldt bought one of the Thousand Islands, had it reshaped into a heart and started building this castle for his wife. Work stopped when she died, and the castle was never finished.
Bottom: Perth's Main Street is lined with restored 19th-century buildings. The town was founded in 1816 as a military settlement.

Cottage Country

About an hour's drive north of Belleville lies the Kawartha Lakes resort region. Bancroft, a small community once known for its uranium mines, now attracts visitors to its annual Rockhound Gemboree, a display of local gemstones and minerals. The area around Peterborough was once the home of prehistoric native tribes, and the black symbols they painted on white rocks and their unusual burial grounds can still be seen. Peterborough lies at the centre of the Kawartha Lakes resort region, which has over 500 lakes and many small hills, called drumlins, deposited by melting glaciers. The Trent-Severn Waterway, which cuts through the small city, has the second-highest lift-lock in the world.

North of the Kawarthas are the rolling hills and forests of the Haliburton Highlands. Over 600 lakes, spectacular fall colours and excellent winter facilities make this area popular year-round. North of Haliburton is Algonquin Park, a vast forested expanse of great

Cottages at Dorset, the southern gateway to Algonquin Park. *Insets: left,* Kirkfield Lift Lock, one of the two hydraulic lift locks on the Trent-Severn Waterway; *right*, petroglyphs, carved by Algonquin Indians between 500 and 1000 years ago

natural beauty covering over 7500 square kilometres (3000 square miles). Reserved for the province in 1893, this park on the edge of the Canadian Shield serves as a living museum of this part of Ontario's natural state. Porcupine, deer, moose, bear, beaver, wolves and many bird species can all be seen by campers who travel by canoe to the interior of the park. Unfortunately the park is in danger: logging and pollution threaten the wildlife of its forests and its 2500 lakes, and environmentalists predict total destruction of its fish and loons by the year 2000 if protective measures are not taken.

Orillia, a pretty town just south of the cottage region of Muskoka, lies at the narrows that link Lake Simcoe and Lake Couchiching. Orillia was a thriving resort town about 1900, just as it is today. Stephen Leacock, a Canadian writer and political economist, poked gentle fun at the town's residents in his best-selling book, *Sunshine Sketches of a Little Town*.

Gravenhurst, a small town north of Orillia on Lake Muskoka, was the birthplace of Norman Bethune, a famous Canadian doctor

Clockwise from above: The Trent Canal, Bobcaygeon; Bala, a small community in the Muskoka area; the demolition derby at Gooderham; Stephen Leacock's lakeshore home in Orillia, now a museum

who made advances in treating turberculosis. In 1936, Bethune operated the world's first mobile blood-transfusion services during the Spanish Civil War, and he later travelled to China to become the chief medical officer for Mao Tse-tung's army. He died there of blood poisoning in 1939 but remains a great hero to the people of China. Many Chinese visitors to Canada journey to Gravenhurst to honour his memory.

Ottawa

When Ottawa, then Bytown, was chosen by Queen Victoria to be the capital of Canada, it was a remote backwoods village of 7500 people, often called "Westminster in the Wilderness." Ottawa is now a cosmopolitan centre with a population of over 300 000 (close

Left: The Rideau Canal at Ottawa. *Top right*: Ballooning over Ottawa. *Above*: The Changing of the Guard on Parliament Hill

to a million with its sister city of Hull across the Ottawa River in the Province of Quebec). Decisions that touch the lives of all Canadians are made in the magnificent limestone Parliament Buildings in downtown Ottawa, and in the city's many other government buildings.

Thanks partly to its natural setting and partly to the efforts of city planners, Ottawa remains a city of rivers, parks, trees and tulips. It boasts one of the longest skating rinks in the world — a seven-kilometre (4.5-mile) stretch of the Rideau Canal that is cleared and maintained for the enjoyment of the city's residents.

In recent years Ottawa has acquired a reputation as a leader in the technology industries, but it remains better known as the site of many museums, galleries, libraries and archives that catalogue and record Canada's history and culture. In addition to major national institutions such as the National Gallery of Canada, the Canadian Museum of Nature, the National Archives and the Canadian War Museum, there are interesting smaller museums like the Bytown Museum, which displays 3500 artifacts used in the building of the Rideau Canal and other early activities, and the Museum of Canadian Scouting which records the development of scouting in Canada.

This brief tour of southern Ontario has unfortunately had to leave countless interesting and charming villages, towns and cities unmentioned. Almost every one has something special to offer: a pretty waterfall, a willow-lined stream; an old grist mill or sawmill or church or school that is now a museum of local history; craft shops, antique shops and markets; a farmhouse turned cozy inn, an abandoned railway station turned art gallery, a barn turned theatre. Any bend in the road can bring a delightful surprise — and it is hardly ever more than a few minutes from one to the next.

Right: **The Niagara Apothecary Museum at Niagara-on-the-Lake.** *Far right*: **Flea market in the village of Aberfoyle.** *Below*: **Wildflowers, Prince Edward County**

Ontario's Northland

Northern Ontario is a very different experience. It is a land of rugged ancient rock and thousands of lakes and the giant forests that gradually give way to scraggly spruce and eventually disappear near the tree line. Overall, it is an area of very cold winters, summers that range from hot to barely warm and crisp autumns.

Even in the more populous southern part, villages and towns can be half a day's drive apart, and the most northern areas can be reached only by canoe, bush plane or train. The Polar Bear Express, a train that runs from Cochrane to Moosonee on James Bay, provides the only land access to that town and to Moose Factory, which lies just off the coast on Moose Island. This section of Ontario attracts hunters, fishermen, people who enjoy isolation and hardy tourists who hope to see the polar bears

Left: Black River Falls, Agawa Canyon. The Algoma Central Railway is the only way into this spectacularly scenic canyon north of Sault Ste. Marie. *Top right*: Kenora is both a pulp and paper town and the holiday headquarters for Lake of the Woods. *Bottom right*: A view of Thunder Bay and the surrounding bluffs

Clockwise from above: **The Terry Fox monument at Thunder Bay was erected near the spot where cancer forced the young runner to end his Marathon of Hope; the International Bridge and canal locks at Sault Ste. Marie; Sioux Narrows, a vacation centre on Lake of the Woods; the Hudson's Bay Company staff house, built in 1847, at Moose Factory**

Several cities in northern Ontario are major centres. Elliot Lake, Sudbury, Wawa and Timmins are all known for their mining activity. Sault Ste. Marie, a major steel producer for Canada, lies at the junction of Lakes Huron and Superior. Its canal system handles more than 100 million tonnes of grain and ore cargo every year.

Island enveloped in mist, Lake Superior Provincial Park.
Inset: **Polar bear off the Hudson Bay shore**

Science North, in Sudbury, is a hands-on museum much like the Science Centre in Toronto. Thunder Bay, with one of the world's highest ski jumps, is a training centre for many of Canada's Olympic skiers. Situated on the northwest shore of Lake Superior, it is close to the centre of Canada. Tonnes of prairie wheat are collected in its huge storage bins for shipment down the Great Lakes and the St. Lawrence Seaway to the world's ports.

Between Thunder Bay and Rainy Lake, Quetico Provincial Park has 1500 kilometres (900 miles) of canoe routes that link up with canoe routes in Minnesota.

Kenora, a forestry and mining centre, just a few minutes from the Manitoba border, is also a popular resort town. Every summer it hosts a seven-day sailing race around the island-studded Lake of the Woods.

Facts
at a Glance

General Information

Creation as a Province: 1867

Origin of Name: Ontario is an Iroquoian word meaning "shining waters" or "beautiful lake."

Provincial Capital: Toronto

Provincial Motto: *Ut incepit fidelis sic permanet*. The Latin words are translated "Loyal she began, loyal she remains."

Provincial Flower: White trillium

Population

Population: 10 084 885 (1991 census)

Largest Cities: Toronto, Ottawa, Hamilton, St. Catharine's-Niagara Falls, London, Kitchener-Waterloo, Windsor, Oshawa, Sudbury, Thunder Bay

Population Distribution: 82.1 percent urban, 17.9 percent rural

Population Density: 10.2 per km² (26.4 per sq. mi.)

Population Growth Rate: 5.5 percent increase from 1981 to 1986, 10.6 percent increase from 1986 to 1991

Year	Population
1851	952 000
1861	1 400 000
1871	1 621 000
1891	2 100 000
1901	2 200 000
1921	2 900 000
1941	3 787 655
1961	6 236 000
1981	8 601 100
1991	10 084 885

Geography

Northern and southern Ontario: Ontario is often viewed as two separate regions, divided by an imaginary line drawn along the Mattawa River, Lake Nipissing, and the French River. The harsh and rocky lands of northern Ontario contain about 10 percent of the population, though they make up almost 90 percent of the land mass of the province. The rich and rolling lands of southern Ontario account for almost 90 percent of the population and 10 percent of the land mass.

Borders: Ontario shares borders with Manitoba on the west and Quebec on the east. The northern border lies along James Bay and Hudson Bay. The southern border lies in the middle of the Great Lakes and the St. Lawrence River; it is shared with the United States.

Highest Point: Ishpatina Ridge, 693 m (2274 ft.)

Lowest Point: Hudson Bay, sea level

Greatest Distances: From north to south, the greatest distance is 1690 km (1050 mi.), and from east to west, the greatest distance is 1609 km (1000 mi.)

Area: 1 068 580 km² (412 611 sq. mi.)

Rank in Area Among the Provinces: Second

Rivers: Principal rivers in northern Ontario are the Moose, Albany, Attawapiskat, Winisk, Severn, Rainy and English. The southern river systems are complemented by many artificial features. The St. Lawrence Seaway includes the St. Lawrence, Welland, and Sault Ste. Marie canals. The Rideau Waterway connects the Ottawa River with Lake Ontario. The Trent-Severn Waterway connects Lake Ontario with Georgian Bay.

Lakes: There are approximately a quarter of a million lakes in Ontario, covering an area of about 177 000 km² (68 000 sq. mi.). Four Great Lakes lie partly in Ontario: Huron, Superior, Ontario, and Erie. Other large lakes are Lake of the Woods, Lake of Bays, Nipigon, Nipissing, Simcoe and St. Clair.

Islands: There are two well-known island groups in Ontario: the Thousand Islands in the St. Lawrence and the Thirty Thousand Islands in Georgian Bay. Less well known and without a collective name are the 14 600 islands in Lake of the Woods. Manitoulin Island in Georgian Bay is thought to be the largest island in the world lying within a freshwater lake.

Topography: Ontario has a typical terrain of rolling hills, plateaus and basins. The most significant landform in southern Ontario is the Niagara Escarpment, a sheer cliff face that cuts northward through the province from Lake Ontario to the Bruce Peninsula. Most of Ontario is covered by the Canadian Shield, a layer of ancient rock.

Climate: Northern Ontario experiences far colder winters than does southern Ontario. The water of the Great Lakes in the south moderates the icy blasts that blow down from the north. Both the northern and southern regions experience four seasons in the year, although the southern climate is generally warmer. Droughts rarely occur in Ontario.

Nature

Trees: The land-clearing pioneers logged much of southern Ontario's original forest, but there are still large untouched tracts in northern Ontario. Many different kinds of trees grow in Ontario, including

Grenadier Pond, High Park, Toronto. Legend has it that during the War of 1812 a group of retreating Grenadiers lost their way in the dark, blundered into this pond and all drowned. No evidence was ever found to support the story, but the name stuck.

maple, birch, beech, basswood, walnut, oak, ash, hickory, poplar, white pine, red cedar, white spruce and tamarack. Some chestnut, magnolia, and sassafras also grow in the south.

Wild Plants: Hundreds of varieties of wild plants grow in Ontario, lining the roads and brightening the forest's floor. Some of the more common plants are the red and white trillium, daisy, dandelion, yarrow, Queen Anne's Lace, milkweed, devil's paintbrush, lily, rose, and iris. Some of the edible wild berries which grow in Ontario are blueberries, raspberries, strawberries, blackberries, cranberries, and gooseberries.

Animals: The forests, fields, and tundra of Ontario are home to many creatures. Some of the larger animals are polar bear, moose, caribou, deer, and black bears. Some of the smaller animals are porcupine, raccoons, rabbits, wolves, fox, beaver, skunk, mink, otter, squirrels, and chipmunks.

Birds: Some of the birds that nest in Ontario are sparrows, finches, robins, crows, eagles, gulls, ducks, geese, woodpeckers, hummingbirds, hawks, quail, partridge, loons, and owls.

Fish: The ten sports fish most often caught and eaten in Ontario are, in order of popularity, walleye, smallmouth bass, yellow perch, northern pike, largemouth bass, rainbow trout, lake trout, brook trout, chinook salmon, and coho salmon.

Government

Ontario's provincial government is led by a premier who is the leader of the political party which holds the most seats in the provincial legislature. Members of the Legislative Assembly are elected by Canadian citizens who are 18 years old or over and residents of Ontario.

The judicial branch of Ontario's government is mostly controlled by the federal government, and most judges are appointed by Ottawa.

Number of cities: 49

Number of towns: 146

Number of townships: 477

Number of Members of Parliament: 99

Number of Senators: 24

Education

Ontario spends about 20 percent of its annual provincial budget on educating its students. All children between the ages of six and sixteen must attend school or receive equivalent education at home. Ontario is now educating almost two million children. As well as the regular public schools, there are government-funded "separate" Roman Catholic schools, and more than 300 French-language elementary and secondary schools.

The province funds almost 50 post-secondary educational institutions.

Some of its major universities are the University of Toronto, York University in Toronto, Queen's University in Kingston, the University of Western Ontario in London, McMaster in Hamilton and the bilingual University of Ottawa.

Economy and Industry

Principal Products

Agriculture: Hay, oats, mixed grains, corn, milk

Manufacturing: Steel, cars, food processing

Natural Resources: Nickel, copper, zinc, uranium, wood

Finance: Ontario is the financial hub of Canada. The Toronto Stock Exchange and many banks handle the monetary needs of the head offices of large corporations.

Tourism: Tourists bring more than $6 billion into Ontario each year. Visitors arrive from all over the world to enjoy the province's varied climate, beautiful scenery, and sports and cultural activities.

Transportation: Ontario's first paved highway was built in 1918, between Hamilton and Toronto. Railways and waterways once provided close to 90 percent of the transport of manufactured goods, but their importance has dwindled, giving way to trucking. Ontario's locks and canals, which include the St. Lawrence Seaway, the Welland

Brockville, one of the first Loyalist settlements in Upper Canada

Canal, the Trent-Severn Waterway, and the locks at Sault Ste. Marie, are among the busiest shipping lanes in the world. The province has hundreds of airfields, of which the largest is Toronto's Pearson International Airport with its three terminals.

Communication: Ontario has about 40 daily newspapers. Of these, the *Toronto Star* has the largest circulation. Hundreds of community newspapers and several ethnic papers are published once a week. About 140 radio stations and some 30 local television stations also keep the public in touch with the news.

Social and Cultural Life

Museums: The city of Toronto has many important museums, including The Royal Ontario Museum, the Sigmund Samuel Canadiana Gallery, the Marine Museum of Upper Canada, the Ontario Science Centre, and the Museum of the Queen's Own Rifles of Canada which is housed in Casa Loma. Some major museums in Ottawa are Bytown Museum, the

National Postal Museum, and the Canadian Ski Museum. Notable museums around the province are the Hastings County Museum in Belleville, the Museum of Northern History in Kirkland Lake, the Ontario Agricultural Museum in Milton, the Niagara Falls Art Gallery and Museum, the Canadian Automotive Museum in Oshawa, and the Peterborough Centennial Museum. Science North, in Sudbury, is a hands-on museum that encourages its visitors to participate in science activities.

Libraries: There are several major libraries in Ontario, including the John Robarts Library, the Thomas Fisher Rare Books Library, and the Metropolitan Toronto Reference Library. The John Robarts Library, housed in a massive $48-million structure, catalogues every book of the enormous University of Toronto collection of more than 4 million volumes. It is the largest collection in Canada and one of the ten largest in North America. Canada's largest military library is in the Canadian Military Institute in Toronto.

Music: Ontario is home to a number of symphony orchestras and youth orchestras. The Toronto Symphony, the London Symphony, and the National Arts Centre Orchestra of Ottawa are perhaps the best known of Ontario's orchestras. During the summer months several well-known music festivals are held in Ontario, in Guelph, Stratford, Ottawa and Peterborough.

Guelph, Stratford, Ottawa, and Peterborough.

Sports and Recreation: Ontario has several professional sports teams, the newest of which is the Raptors of the National Basketball Association (NBA). Its chief baseball team is the Toronto Blue Jays, and its main hockey teams are the Toronto Maple Leafs and the Ottawa Senators. The top football teams are the Hamilton Tiger Cats, the Ottawa Rough Riders and the Toronto Argonauts.

Horse-racing is popular in Ontario. The Queen's Plate held in June at Toronto's Woodbine Racetrack brings excitement to the beginning of the racing season. Major racetracks are located in Ottawa, Hamilton, Sudbury and Peterborough.

Tennis, golf, swimming, boating, fishing, bicycling, cross-country skiing, downhill skiing and skating are all major sports in Ontario.

Ontario's more than 250 provincial and six national parks, and its over a quarter of a million lakes draw thousands of visitors every year. Camping, whitewater rafting and hiking are all vacation activities that many people enjoy, year after year, in the outdoor playground of Ontario.

Historic Sites and Landmarks:

Casa Loma, in Toronto, is North America's largest castle. It was built by the industrialist Sir Henry Pellat in 1914 at enormous cost, with materials such as oak, teak and marble. The château-like castle has 98 rooms, and several secret passages.

Gibson House, in Toronto, is a red brick Georgian house that has been restored and set up to reflect the busy rural life of early Ontario. The house was built in 1849 by David Gibson, who was a participant in the Rebellion of 1837.

Huron County Pioneer Museum, in Goderich, displays and demonstrates activities of early Ontario village life, including flour milling and maple sugar making. A Victorian street scene displays original storefronts and early Ontario artifacts.

Muskoka Pioneer Museum, in Huntsville, highlights aspects of pioneer life in Ontario between 1860 and 1910. Included are a reconstructed pioneer house, church and schoolhouse.

Nancy Island Historic Site, on Nancy Island at Wasaga Beach, marks the place where HMS *Nancy* was sunk by the Americans during the War of 1812. The charred remains of the ship were salvaged and are now on display in the museum. The museum also displays models of ships which sailed the Great Lakes during the 1800s.

Old Fort Erie, originally built in the mid-1700s, was destroyed and rebuilt several times by both Americans and Canadians. It has since been restored and is now a working model of a military fort.

Old Fort Henry, near Kingston, is a living museum of British and Canadian military history. Parades, drills, salutes and ceremonial retreats help to recreate nineteenth-century military life. The fort's 126 rooms have been restored to appear as they did when in use by British garrisons over 150 years ago. Collections of military and naval equipment include items salvaged from vessels engaged in the War of 1812.

Old Fort William, near Thunder Bay, is a reconstruction of the original western headquarters of the North West Company. The post contains blacksmith, tinsmith, gunsmith, tailor and cooper workshops, a native encampment and a site where large birchbark canoes are made. There is also a farm, a dairy and a naval yard.

The Parliament Buildings, in Ottawa, are Gothic limestone buildings with green copper roofs. The original Centre Block, except for the library, was destroyed by fire in 1916. It was reconstructed in the original form, and its Peace Tower, which is the outstanding feature of the Block, dominates the city from its vantage point on Parliament Hill. The Peace Tower is dedicated to Canada's war dead and contains inscriptions of their names, poems commemorating the First World War and a set of bells.

Sainte-Marie Among the Hurons, near Midland, is a carefully reconstructed village containing buildings and displays reflecting the lives of a handful of Jesuit missionaries and the Huron Indians who lived in the area in the 1600s.

Upper Canada Village, in Morrisburg, recreates the way of life of a village in Upper Canada in the 1800s. More than 30 buildings make up the village, including houses, churches, mills, taverns, and shops. Each building has been furnished to portray accurately early life in the St. Lawrence Valley. Visitors to the village can observe typical daily activities of Ontario's early settlers, such as breadmaking and cheese-making.

Other Interesting Places to Visit:

Amherstburg is an old Loyalist settlement in southern Ontario, where British settlers made their homes, in 1796.

Fort Malden was a major post in Upper Canada. It was burned to the ground by the Americans during the War of 1812, but was later restored and occupied by the British. The fort was a main base during the Rebellion of 1837.

Bowmanville Museum contains toys that Canadian children played with over 100 years ago. The museum is a large house, furnished in Victorian style.

Brantford, a small city in southern Ontario, contains many historically important museums, houses, sites and artifacts. It was here that Joseph Brant relocated Loyalist Iroquois from New York. One museum contains artifacts of this settlement and a memorial to Joseph Brant and the Six Nations tribes. Bell Memorial and the Bell Homestead commemorate Alexander Graham Bell's invention of the telephone, which took place in Brantford.

Joseph Brant Museum in Burlington is a replica of Brant's last home, which he built on this site about 1800.

Dundurn Castle in Hamilton is a magnificent mansion which the City of Hamilton restored to its original splendour. Built in 1834, it was the home of Sir Allan MacNab, a lawyer who was prime minister of the United Province of Canada from 1854 to 1856.

Elliot Lake Mining and Nuclear Museum displays models of uranium mines and depicts uranium processing. The museum also contains relics of the lumber industry's early days.

Martyrs' Shrine, near Midland, commemorates the six Jesuit missionaries who were killed there in the late 1640s.

Moose Factory Island, near Moosonee, was a strategic trading post of the Hudson's Bay Company. French and British fought over it until 1713, when it became part of the British lands in North America. On the island is a museum that depicts early life in the fur trade.

Tin House Court, Ottawa

Parkwood is the fabulous Oshawa mansion of R.S. McLaughlin, the auto manufacturer who became chairman of General Motors of Canada.

Pump House Steam Museum in Kingston is the world's largest working model of a pumping station.

Serpent Mounds Provincial Park on the shore of Rice Lake contains a mysterious mound 60 m (200 ft.) long. It is now known that a native group raised this and other burial mounds about 2000 years ago.

The Ukrainian Historical and Cultural Museum in Timmins shows something of the lives of Ukrainian immigrants who settled in northern Ontario.

Important Dates

1612	French explorer Etienne Brulé is the first European to enter the area that is now Ontario
1620	The Hurons become intermediaries in the fur trade
1638	Half of the Huron tribe dies in an epidemic of smallpox brought by Europeans
1648	The Iroquois attack and almost completely destroy the Hurons
1673	Fort Cataraqui (later Fort Frontenac), the first permanent European settlement, is built on the future site of Kingston; The Hudson's Bay Company completes Moose Factory
1713	The Treaty of Utrecht confirms British possession of Rupert's Land
1763	The Seven Years' War ends, and the British take over New France
1774	The British Parliament passes the Quebec Act, defining the boundaries of the Quebec colony which at that time includes the Great Lakes area
1775	American rebels unsuccessfully invade Quebec
1783	The Treaty of Paris ends the American War of Independence and thirteen of Britain's American colonies become the United States of America; thousands of Loyalists move north into Canada
1784	Chief Joseph Brant and his Loyalist Mohawks receive a large grant of land along the Grand River
1791	The British Parliament passes the Constitutional Act dividing Quebec into two parts: Upper Canada and Lower Canada
1792	Upper Canada's first Legislative Assembly is opened by Lieutenant-Governor Simcoe
1803	Colonel Thomas Talbot founds a large settlement in southwestern Ontario
1805	The British purchase the lakefront at Burlington Bay from the Mississauga Indians
1812	The United States declares war on Great Britain
1813	Indian leader Tecumseh is killed in the Battle of Moraviantown
1814	The War of 1812 ends; both Americans and British return the lands they have taken
1817	The Rush-Bagot Agreement is signed limiting arms on the Great Lakes
1829	The Welland Canal is completed
1832	The Rideau Canal is completed
1837	William Lyon Mackenzie leads an unsuccessful rebellion
1840	The British Parliament passes the Act of Union joining Upper and Lower Canada into the United Province of Canada
1843	The Cornwall Canal is finished, completing a water route from Montreal to Sault Ste. Marie

1848	The first "responsible" government is formed, with the premier and ministers chosen from the elected members of the assembly
1850	Lumbering, Ontario's first large-scale industry, begins to flourish
1850	The Toronto Stock Exchange is established
1853	The Great Western Railway between Hamilton and Niagara Falls opens
1854	A Reciprocity Treaty is negotiated with the United States
1856	The Grand Trunk railway is completed between Montreal and Toronto
1857	Queen Victoria names Ottawa the capital of the United Provinces of Canada
1860	The American Civil War breaks out, and British troops arrive in case Canada should be drawn into the war
1863	The Scott Act is passed, establishing a dual system of publicly financed schools that include separate Roman Catholic schools
1865	The Reciprocity Treaty with the United States is cancelled
1866	Fenians, a group of Irish-American extremists, attack Ridgeway, near Fort Erie
1867	Confederation unites four provinces — Nova Scotia, New Brunswick, Quebec and Ontario — to form the Dominion of Canada
1867	John Sandfield Macdonald becomes Ontario's first premier
1872	Oliver Mowat becomes premier
1876	Dr. Emily Stowe founds the Toronto Women's Literary Club, an organization dedicated to improving women's rights
1879	The federal government develops a "National Policy" that includes high tariffs to protect Ontario and Quebec industries
1883	Nickel is discovered near Sudbury; The Great Western Railway merges with the Grand Trunk
1889	Federal legislation extends Ontario's northwestern boundary beyond Rat Portage (now Kenora)
1893	Algonquin Park is established
1896	Niagara Falls hydroelectric plant opens

Early church, Toronto

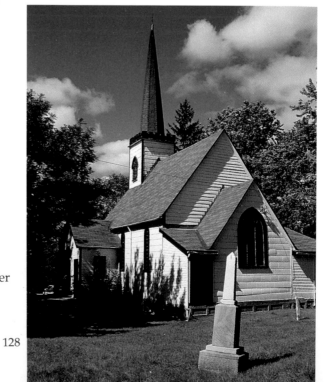

1905	After many years of Liberal government Ontario elects a Conservative government led by James P. Whitney
1906	The Hydro-Electric Power Commission is formed to provide Ontarians with cheap power
1912	Ontario's Department of Education bans the use of French for teaching beyond an early level in the province's schools; Ontario's northern boundary is extended to Hudson Bay
1914	Ontario adopts Canada's first Workmen's Compensation Act; British declaration takes Canada to war
1917	Ontario grants women the right to vote in provincial elections
1919	The United Farmers of Ontario win the provincial election; Ontario votes itself "dry"
1921	Agnes Macphail of Grey County becomes the first woman elected to the Canadian House of Commons
1927	Teaching in French is again allowed in eastern Ontario schools
1933	The Great Depression forces half a million Ontarians to depend on government relief
1934	Mitchell Hepburn becomes premier of Ontario
1937	A strike at the General Motors factory in Oshawa is settled by management's
	first-ever agreement with a union, the United Auto Workers
1939	Canada declares war on Germany
1943	The Conservative Party led by George Drew is elected
1952	Uranium is discovered in central Ontario, near Algoma
1954	The St. Lawrence Seaway Treaty is signed, and construction begins; Hurricane Hazel wreaks havoc through southern Ontario
1961	John Robarts becomes premier
1963	Ontario joins the National Pension Plan
1971	William Davis becomes premier
1974	Pauline McGibbon becomes the province's — and the country's — first woman lieutenant-governor
1982	Queen Elizabeth II signs Canada's new constitutional accord in Ottawa
1985	Liberal David Peterson becomes premier
1990	Ontario elects its first NDP government, led by Bob Rae
1995	Mike Harris leads the Conservatives to victory on the promise of sweeping social reforms and government restraint
1996	Toronto's Yonge Street turns 200 years old; the longest street in the world, according to the *Guinness Book of Records*, stretches 1886 km (1,172 mi.) to Rainy River, Ontario

Lincoln Alexander

Margaret Atwood

Frederick Banting

Pierre Berton

Important People

Lincoln Alexander (1922-   ), born in Toronto of West Indian parents; lawyer, politician, lieutenant-governor; served in the Second World War, then practised law until elected to Parliament; federal minister of labour 1979-80; lieutenant-governor of Ontario 1985 to 1991

Elizabeth Arden (1884-1966), born Florence Nightingale Graham in Woodbridge; moved to New York at age 25 and worked at a cosmetics firm; opened her own beauty salon under the name of Elizabeth Arden and turned it into a hugely successful cosmetics empire

Margaret Atwood (1939-   ), born in Ottawa; poet, novelist, critic; first published book of poetry, 1961, first published novel, 1969; has won two Governor General awards: for *The Circle Game* (poetry) in 1966 and for her novel *The Handmaid's Tale* in 1985

Robert Baldwin (1804-1858), born in York (Toronto); politician; co-premier of the United Province of Canada 1842-43 and 1848-51; leader of the movement for responsible government

Frederick Banting (1891-1941), born in Alliston; physician and medical researcher; discovered insulin as a treatment for diabetes in 1921 with three colleagues, **Charles Best**, **James Collip**, and **J. MacLeod**; co-recipient (with Best) of the 1923 Nobel Prize for chemistry

Adam Beck (1857-1925), born in Baden; provincial cabinet minister responsible for creating Ontario Hydro in 1906; guided the project at Niagara Falls until it became one of the world's largest sources of energy

Pierre Berton (1920-   ), born in Whitehorse, Yukon, lives in Ontario; prolific non-fiction writer best known for his popular histories, including *The War of 1812*, *The National Dream* and *The Last Spike*, *Klondike* and *The Great Depression*; three-time winner of Governor General's Award

Norman Bethune (1890-1939), born in Gravenhurst; a dedicated doctor who believed in and supported humanitarian causes; fought against tuberculosis with new treatments; operated the world's first mobile blood-transfusion service in the Spanish Civil War; died while serving as chief medical officer of Mao Tse-tung's army in China

Billy Bishop (1894-1956), born in Owen Sound; flying ace; winner of Victoria Cross; shot down 72 enemy planes during the First World War, ranking third among all the aces of the war

Joseph Brant (1742-1807), American-born Mohawk chief

who gave Brantford its name; principal chief of the Six Nations (the Iroquois Confederacy); fought for the British during the Seven Years' War and the American Revolution, then brought his Loyalist people to Canada to a reserve on the Grand River; in later life translated parts of the Bible and the Book of Common Prayer into Mohawk

Sir Isaac Brock (1769-1812), born in Guernsey; hero of the War of 1812; responsible for the strategy that resulted in early victories at Michilimackinac, Detroit and Queenston, earned a knighthood for his victory at Detroit but died at Queenston Heights before hearing of the award

Brockhaus, Bertram (1918-   ), Alberta-born scientist; after studying at the universities of British Columbia and Toronto, worked for 12 years at the Chalk River Nuclear Laboratories, then as professor of physics at McMaster University; co-winner of 1994 Nobel Prize for Physics

George Brown (1818-1880), Scottish-born journalist, politician, Father of Confederation; founder and publisher of the Toronto *Globe*; leader of the Reform Party in the 1850s and 1860s; his willingness to form an alliance with Conservative leader John A. Macdonald made Confederation possible

Shirley Carr, born at Niagara Falls; union leader; member of the Canadian Union of Public Employees, she served in several executive positions at the provincial and national levels; elected president of the Canadian Labour Congress in 1986, the first woman to hold the position

Brock Chisolm (1896-1971), born in Oakville; psychiatrist; helped set up the World Health Organization and was its first director general; fought disease, poverty and ignorance around the world

Lionel Conacher (1900-1954), born in Toronto; considered by many to be Canada's greatest athlete; excellent in baseball, boxing, football, hockey and lacrosse; played on winning Grey Cup and Stanley Cup teams; elected to Ontario Legislature in 1937 and to Parliament in 1949

Donald Creighton (1902-1979), born in Toronto; historian, author; winner of two Governor General's Awards (1952, 1955) for his two-volume biography of Sir John A. Macdonald; named a Companion of the Order of Canada

Robertson Davies (1913-1995), born in Thamesville; writer, professor; popular newspaper columnist for many years and award-winning playwright;

Billy Bishop

Isaac Brock

George Brown

Brock Chisholm

Robertson Davies

Mazo de la Roche

Glenn Gould

Graham Greene

now best known and widely acclaimed for novel trilogies published in the seventies and eighties

Mazo de la Roche (1879-1961), born in Newmarket; novelist; achieved fame with her third novel, *Jalna*, which won the Atlantic Monthly Prize in 1927; wrote 16 more novels about the Whiteoak family, owners of the Jalna farm; the series was an international best seller

Dionne Quintuplets
(1934-   ), born in Callander; Yvonne, Annette, Cécile, Emilie and Marie were the world's first quintuplets to survive; raised for nine years under the protection of the Ontario Government, they were a major tourist attraction

Timothy Eaton (1834-1907), Irish-born founder of Eaton's chain of department stores; initiated new business practices, such as fixed prices on goods, cash payment, money back guarantees and mail-order service

Celia Franca (1921-   ), English-born founder of the National Ballet of Canada; organized the original 29 dancers of the company and was its principal dancer for many years

Northrop Frye (1912-1991), distinguished literary scholar affiliated with the University of Toronto's Victoria College for

many years; world-wide reputation as a brilliant literary critic

Glenn Gould (1932-1982), born in Toronto; pianist; made his concert debut with the Toronto Symphony Orchestra at age 14; gave up the concert stage in 1964 to devote himself to recording; made more than 80 records, with the most famous being Bach's *Goldberg Variations*

Graham Greene born on the Six Nations Reserve; prominent stage, film and television actor; best known for his performance in the play *Dry Lips Oughtta Move to Kapuskasing*, for which he won a Dora Mavor Moore Award for best actor, and for his role as Kicking Bird in the film *Dances with Wolves*, which earned him an Academy Award nomination.

Wayne Gretzky (1961-   ), Brantford-born hockey star; played with the Edmonton Oilers from 1978 to 1988, then with the Los Angeles Kings; smashed scoring record after scoring record and won just about every award and trophy it was possible to win

Group of Seven, group of artists officially formed in Toronto in the 1920s; main founders were Ontario painters **Lawren Harris** and **J.E.H. Mac-Donald**; the other original members, most of whom were either born in Ontario or spent much of their working life there, were Franklin Carmichael, Frank Johnston, Arthur Lismer, Frederick Varley and A.Y. Jackson; the group disbanded in the early 1930s but its impact on Canadian art was enormous

Josiah Henson (1789-1883), an American-born black slave, who escaped to Canada in 1830 on the "underground railroad"; founded a settlement for runaway slaves near Dresden; experiences related in his autobiography are thought to be the basis for Harriet Beecher Stowe's famous novel *Uncle Tom's Cabin*

James Hillier (1915-   ), born in Brantford; scientist; designed and built the first electron microscope, which is now used all over the world by researchers because of its tremendous magnifying power

Adelaide Hoodless (1857-1910), born in south Dumfries; founder of the first Women's Institute, an organization, now worldwide, devoted to educating women for motherhood and household management; helped organize the Canadian YWCA, the National Council of Women of Canada and the Victorian Order of Nurses

Bobby Hull (1939-   ), born in Pointe Anne; great hockey star who has won almost every hockey award possible; played for the Chicago Black Hawks for 15 years, then with the Winnipeg Jets; scored more than 900 goals during his career

Ferguson Jenkins (1943-   ), born at Chatham; baseball player; considered one of the game's great pitchers; won 284 games and struck out 3192 batters during his career; first Canadian ever inducted into the Baseball Hall of Fame

Norman Jewison (1926-   ), born in Toronto; film director and producer; his films include *Moonstruck*, *Jesus Christ Superstar*, *Fiddler on the Roof*, and *In the Heat of the Night* which won the Academy Award for best picture of 1967

Pauline Johnson (1862-1913), born on the Six Nations Reserve; poet and entertainer; gained international fame with stage recitations of her poetry, which celebrated nature and her Indian heritage

John J. Kelso (1864-1935); social reformer; in 1887, founded the Toronto Humane Society for the prevention of cruelty to animals and children; in 1891, organized the Toronto Children's Aid Society; later helped set up similar organizations in other provinces

William Lyon Mackenzie King (1874-1950), born in Kitchener; politician; was Liberal prime minister for over 20 years,

Adelaide Hoodless

Bobby Hull

Pauline Johnson

W. L. Mackenzie King

Bora Laskin

Tom Longboat

John McCrae

John A. Macdonald

through most of the 1920s and from 1935 to 1948; although the grandson of the fiery William Lyon Mackenzie, he was cautious, shrewd, and a skilful negotiator

Bora Laskin (1912-1984), born in Fort William; lawyer, judge; appointed to the Supreme Court of Canada in 1970 and named chief justice in 1973; known as a civil libertarian and an expert on constitutional and labour law; died in office

Stephen Leacock (1869-1944), humorist, political economist; head of the department of political science at McGill University from 1908 to 1936; published 57 books, the most famous of which is *Sunshine Sketches of a Little Town*, based on recollections of his boyhood in Orillia

Tom Longboat (1887-1949), born on the Six Nations Reserve; distance runner; became a national sports hero when he won the Boston Marathon in 1907 in record time; went on to win many more races and set many records

John McCrae (1872-1918), born in Guelph; physician, poet; served as a medical officer in France during the First World War; wrote the most famous of all war poems, ''In Flanders Fields''

John A. Macdonald (1815-1891) lawyer, politician, first prime minister of Canada; chief spokesman for Confederation in the years 1864-67 and main designer of the new nation's constitution; his vision of Canada involved expansion from sea to sea, a transcontinental railway and the development of the country's industries; as prime minister from 1867 to 1873 and 1878 to 1891, he achieved the realization of that vision

John McIntosh (1777-1845), farmer; an American who settled on a farm at what is now Dundela, McIntosh grew crunchy and sweet red apples from which all McIntosh apples have descended

Alexander Mackenzie (1822-1892), politician, prime minister 1873-78; his two main achievements as prime minister were the establishment of the Supreme Court of Canada and the introduction of the secret ballot

William Lyon Mackenzie (1795-1861), Scottish-born newspaper editor, politician and rebel; first mayor of Toronto, 1834-35; led the Rebellion of 1837 in Upper Canada and fled to the United States when it failed; returned to Canada in 1849

Robert Samuel McLaughlin (1871-1972), born at Enniskillen; industrialist; expanded his father's Oshawa-based carriage-making business into the McLaughlin Motor Car Company in 1907; sold the company to General Motors in 1918 and was chairman of General Motors of Canada until his death

Agnes Macphail (1890-1954), born in Proton Township; politician, champion of the underprivileged; in 1921 became the first woman elected to the House of Commons, and remained the only female there for the next 14 years; defeated in 1940, she won a seat in the provincial legislature three years later

Clara Brett Martin (c. 1872-1923), born in Toronto; lawyer; in 1897 after many struggles, became the first woman lawyer in Canada and the British Empire, paving the way for other women to pursue this career

Hart Massey (1823-1896), born in Cobourg; manufacturer, philanthropist; founder of the hugely successful farm implement company known for many years as Massey-Harris, later as Massey-Ferguson; built Massey Hall for Toronto. One of his grandsons, **Vincent Massey** (1887-1967), became the country's first Canadian-born Governor General in 1952. Another grandson, **Raymond Massey** (1896-1983), was a well-known stage, film and TV actor

William Hamilton Merritt (1793-1862), businessman, politician; organized the building of the Welland Canal, in order to create a waterway from Lake Erie to Lake Ontario; he pressed for the completion of the St. Lawrence Canal system, which provided a navigable waterway from the Great Lakes to the Atlantic Ocean

Sir Oliver Mowat (1820-1903), born in Kingston; politician, Father of Confederation; as premier of Ontario for a record 24 years, was a champion of provincial rights; lieutenant-governor of Ontario from 1897 until his death

James Naismith (1861-1939), born in Almonte; the inventor of basketball, he used peach baskets nailed to a gymnasium's balcony in the first games, hence the name

Lester B. Pearson (1897-1972), born in Toronto; diplomat, politician; ambassador to the United States 1945-46; negotiated Canada's membership in NATO; president of the UN General Assembly 1952-53; winner of the Nobel Peace Prize in 1957 for his efforts in defusing the Suez Crisis; prime minister of Canada from 1963-68

Christopher Plummer (1929-   ), born in Toronto; actor; has starred on stage and in films on both sides of the

Alexander Mackenzie

Agnes Macphail

Oliver Mowat

Lester Pearson

Egerton Ryerson

John Graves Simcoe

Emily Stowe

Roy Thomson

Atlantic; roles have ranged from Hamlet and Macbeth to Captain Von Trapp in *The Sound of Music*

John Polanyi (1929-   ); scientist; came to Canada in 1952 and has been associated with the University of Toronto since 1956; shared the Nobel Prize for Chemistry in 1986

Raffi (1948-   ), Egyptian-born singer; began his career as a folksinger in Toronto coffee-houses and is now one of North America's most popular children's entertainers

Egerton Ryerson (1803-1882), born near Vittoria; Methodist minister; as superintendent of education from 1844 to 1876, he worked to achieve free elementary schooling for all Ontario children

Laura Secord (1775-1868), American-born Loyalist; during the War of 1812, walked from Queenston to Beaver Dams to warn British troops of a planned American attack

John Graves Simcoe (1752-1806), born in England; first governor of Upper Canada, 1791-96; founder of York, which is now Toronto; provided for the gradual end to slavery in Ontario. His wife, **Elizabeth Simcoe** (1762–1850) accompanied him to Upper Canada where she made many sketches and kept a diary that provides fascinating glimpses of life in the young colony

Emily Stowe (1831-1903), born in Norwich; first Canadian woman doctor, suffragist; graduated from an American medical college in 1867 and set up a Toronto practice although not granted a licence to practice there until 1880; helped found Ontario's first women's suffrage group; Her daughter, **Augusta Stowe-Cullen** was the first woman to graduate from a Canadian medical school; led the Ontario suffrage movement for many years

Tecumseh (1768-1813), American-born Shawnee chief, hero of the War of 1812; he and his followers played a major role in early British victories, especially the capture of Detroit; fought with great courage until he was killed in the Battle of Moravian-town

Roy Thomson (1894-1976), born in Toronto; media giant; after starting out by setting up a radio station in North Bay in 1931, came to own a vast number of radio and TV stations and newspapers; moved to Britain in the 1950s, where he was made a baronet, Lord Thomson of Fleet

Tom Thomson (1877-1917), born in Claremont; Ontario painter who was a forerunner of the Group of Seven; drowned under mysterious circumstances in Algonquin Park before the artists' group was formed

Catherine Parr Traill (1802-1899), born in England; author of accounts of pioneering in Upper Canada, including *The Canadian Settler's Guide* and *The Backwoods of Canada*. Her sister **Susanna Moodie** (1803-1885), was also a pioneer author, best known for *Roughing it in the Bush*, an account of her experiences as a settler in the backwoods

Thomas Willson (1860-1915), born in Princeton; inventor; earned the nickname Carbide Willson because of his discovery in 1892 of how to make carbide and acetylene; established the first Canadian hydroelectric plant; advocated Canadian use of Niagara Falls power

Neil Young (1945-   ), born in Toronto; singer, songwriter; with Stephen Stills, formed one of America's first supergroups, Buffalo Springfield; since 1969 has performed solo and with Crosby Stills Nash and Young, achieving several gold-record sales awards

Catherine Parr Traill

Premiers of Ontario since Confederation

John Sandfield Macdonald	Liberal-Conservative	1867-71
Edward Blake	Liberal	1871-72
Oliver Mowat	Liberal	1872-96
Arthur Sturgis Hardy	Liberal	1896-99
George William Ross	Liberal	1899-1905
James Pliny Whitney	Conservative	1905-14
William Howard Hearst	Conservative	1914-19
Ernest Charles Drury	United Farmers of Ontario	1919-23
George Howard Ferguson	Conservative	1923-30
George Stewart Henry	Conservative	1930-34
Mitchell Frederick Hepburn	Liberal	1934-42
Gordon Daniel Conant	Liberal	1942-43
Harry Corwin Nixon	Liberal	1943
George Alexander Drew	Conservative	1943-48
Thomas Laird Kennedy	Conservative	1948-49
Leslie Miscampbell Frost	Conservative	1949-61
John Parmenter Robarts	Conservative	1961-71
William Grenville Davis	Conservative	1971-85
Frank Miller	Conservative	1985
David Robert Peterson	Liberal	1985-90
Robert Rae	New Democratic Party	1990-95
Michael Harris	Conservative	1995-

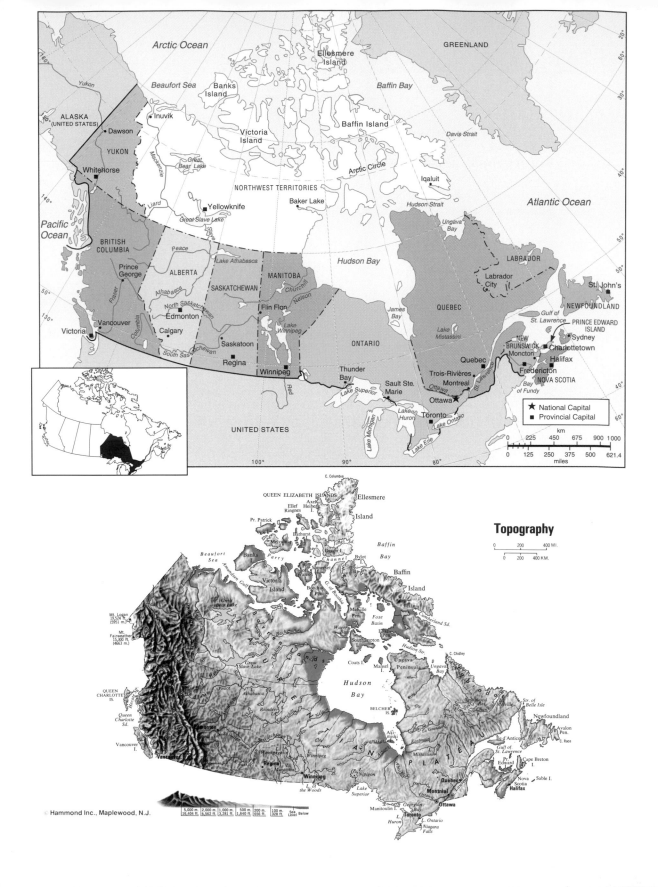

Arctic Ocean

GREENLAND

Ellesmere
Island

Beaufort Sea   Banks
Island   Baffin Bay

ALASKA
(UNITED STATES)   • Inuvik   Victoria   Baffin Island
                                     Island   Davis Strait
      • Dawson

YUKON   Arctic Circle   Atlantic Ocean

  Whitehorse   Iqaluit

                      NORTHWEST TERRITORIES

Pacific   • Yellowknife   Baker Lake   Hudson Strait
Ocean   Great Slave Lake   Ungava
                                                                                  Bay
                                                                                            LABRADOR

       BRITISH   Labrador
       COLUMBIA   Peace   City   St. John's
                                   Lake Athabasca   NEWFOUNDLAND
     Prince   ALBERTA   SASKATCHEWAN   MANITOBA   Hudson Bay   QUEBEC   PRINCE EDWARD
     George   ISLAND
                    Athabasca   North Saskatchewan   James   Gulf of   Sydney
  Vancouver   Edmonton   Flin Flon   Nelson   Bay   St. Lawrence   NEW
Victoria   Calgary   Lake   Lake   BRUNSWICK Charlottetown
                                    Saskatoon   Winnipeg   Mistassini   Montreal   Moncton   Halifax
          Columbia   South Saskatchewan   Regina   ONTARIO   Quebec   Fredericton   NOVA SCOTIA
                                  Winnipeg   Thunder   Trois-Rivières   Bay
                          Red   Bay   Sault Ste.   Montreal   of Fundy
                                                              Marie   Ottawa   St. Lawrence
                                        Lake Superior   Ottawa ★
UNITED STATES   Lake Michigan   Lake Huron   Toronto   Lake Ontario
                                                                                      ★ National Capital
                                          Lake Erie   ■ Provincial Capital

                                                                     km
                                                        0 225 450 675 900 1000
                                                        0 125 250 375 500 621.4
                                                                     miles

Topography

© Hammond Inc., Maplewood, N.J.

5,000 m. 2,000 m. 1,000 m. 500 m. 200 m. 100 m. Sea
16,404 ft. 6,562 ft. 3,281 ft. 1,640 ft. 656 ft. 328 ft. Level Below

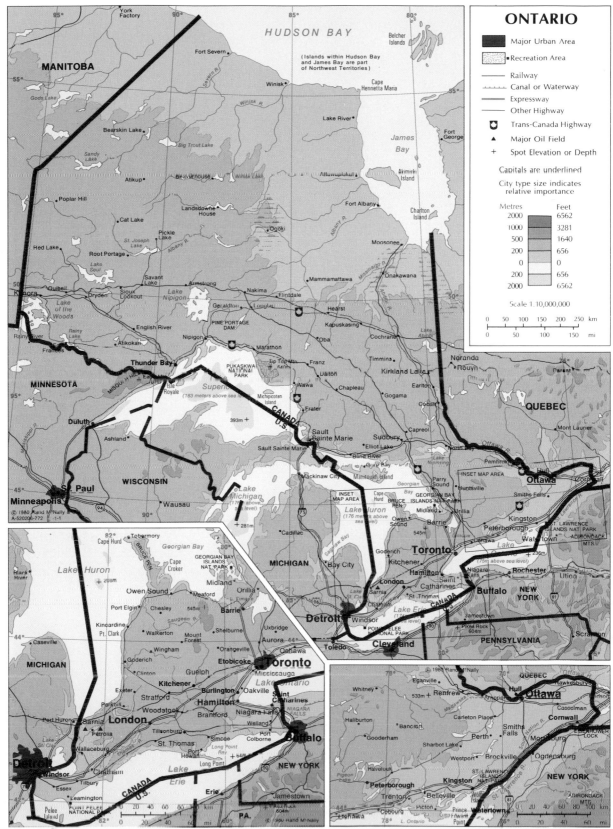

ONTARIO

- ◼ Major Urban Area
- ▨ Recreation Area
- —— Railway
- ┉┉ Canal or Waterway
- ═══ Expressway
- —— Other Highway
- ⬡ Trans-Canada Highway
- ▲ Major Oil Field
- + Spot Elevation or Depth

Capitals are underlined

City type size indicates relative importance

Metres	Feet
2000	6562
1000	3281
500	1640
200	656
0	0
200	656
2000	6562

Scale 1:10,000,000

0 50 100 150 200 250 km
0 50 100 150 mi

© Rand McNally.

AVERAGE ANNUAL RAINFALL

The southern parts of Ontario are wetter than the northern.

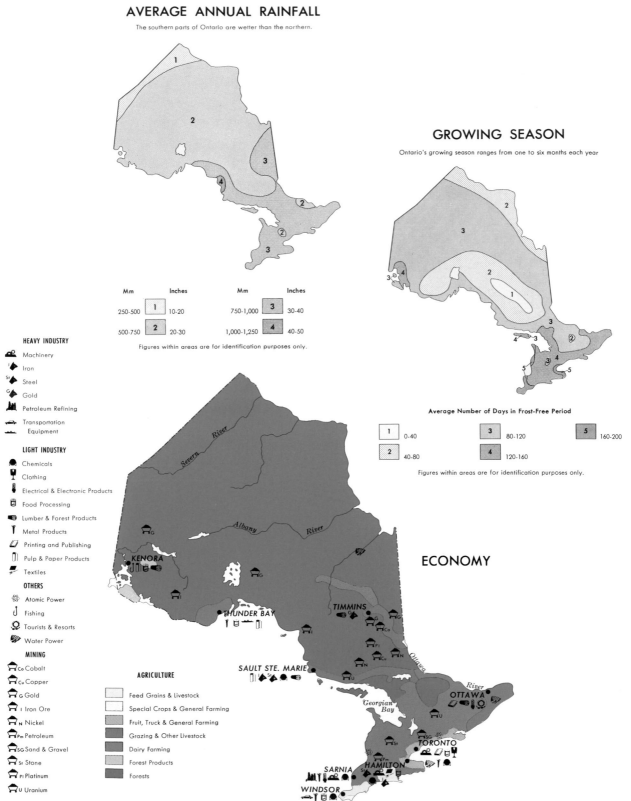

Mm	Inches		Mm	Inches
250-500	**1** 10-20		750-1,000	**3** 30-40
500-750	**2** 20-30		1,000-1,250	**4** 40-50

Figures within areas are for identification purposes only.

GROWING SEASON

Ontario's growing season ranges from one to six months each year

Average Number of Days in Frost-Free Period

1	0-40	**3**	80-120	**5**	160-200
2	40-80	**4**	120-160		

Figures within areas are for identification purposes only.

HEAVY INDUSTRY
Machinery
Iron
Steel
Gold
Petroleum Refining
Transportation Equipment

LIGHT INDUSTRY
Chemicals
Clothing
Electrical & Electronic Products
Food Processing
Lumber & Forest Products
Metal Products
Printing and Publishing
Pulp & Paper Products
Textiles

OTHERS
Atomic Power
Fishing
Tourists & Resorts
Water Power

MINING
Co Cobalt
Cu Copper
G Gold
I Iron Ore
N Nickel
Pm Petroleum
SG Sand & Gravel
St Stone
Pl Platinum
U Uranium

AGRICULTURE
Feed Grains & Livestock
Special Crops & General Farming
Fruit, Truck & General Farming
Grazing & Other Livestock
Dairy Farming
Forest Products
Forests

ECONOMY

KENORA

THUNDER BAY

TIMMINS

SAULT STE. MARIE

Severn River

Albany River

Ottawa River

Georgian Bay

OTTAWA

TORONTO

HAMILTON

SARNIA

WINDSOR

Index

About the Author

Kathryn Mackay writes textbooks, poetry, plays, articles, children's books and educational software. She is a correspondent for the *Toronto Star* and has worked closely with several ministries of education on the development of learning materials. As well, she has taught a wide range of subjects at the elementary, secondary and college levels.

Picture Acknowledgments

Abbreviations for location on page are, alone or in combination: T=Top, M=Middle, B=Bottom, L=Left, R=Right, I=Inset, BG=Background.

Front cover, 6, 8–9, 11R, 14, 16R, 17(all), 19I, 28(both), 44(all), 45TL, 51TL, 51B(both), 53(both), 62R, 66, 70I, 71, 72B, 78B, 81L, 95L(both), 98I, 99TL, 101TR, 101TL, 102(all), 103T, 103BL, 107I, 108I, 109TR, 111(all), 112T, 112BL, 112BR, 118(tree and flower), 128, **Bill Ivy**; 2–3, © Robert Smith/ **Superstock**; 4, Alan Briere/**Superstock**; 5, © Stephan Poulin/**Superstock**; 11L, R. Hartmier/**First Light**; 12L, 14I, © William Reynolds/**Superstock**; 12R, © P. Van Rhijn/**Superstock**; 13L, 80I, © Jerry Kobalenko/**First Light**; 13R, 19, 70, 80, 101B, 117, © Derek Trask/**The Stock Market Inc., Toronto**; 16L, 94R, 99BR, © **Henry Kalen, Winnipeg**; 20 (58. 44. 18), **Glenbow Archives**; 23 (86757), 24I (76024), **National Museum**; 24, 32TL, 32B, 47B, 58T (T15394), 58B (T16587), 136MT, **Metro Toronto Reference Library**; 26 (C2401), 29 (C16833), 32TL (C96361), 32TR (C2001), 35 (C41502), 36 (C21304), 38TM (C31493), 38B (C4782), 39 (C18737), 47TL (C32), 47R (C12632), 56 (C16551), 59 (C14114), 77 (C11878), 97L (PA49893), 130MB (C7516), 130B (C31983), 131T, 131MT (C9553), 131MB, 131B (C59705), 132T (C31986), 132MT (C5482), 133MT (PA 50500), 133B (C387), 134T (PA53715), 134MT (C14090), 134MB (C19919), 135T (C96), 135MT (C19919), 135MB (PA28973), 135B (C10435), 136MB (C9480), 136B (PA52566), 137T (C22884), **National Archives of Canada**; 34, 57, **Confederation Life Collection**; 38TL (S.38.74), 41L (S.2996), 41M (S.13458), 41R (S.9108), 43BL (S.15001), 49 (S.12008), 133T (S4332), 136T (S623), **Ontario Archives**; 43T, **Toronto Transit Commission Archives**; 43BR (SC244-2534), 48T (James Collection, #1830), 48B (Department of Health Collection, #246), **City of Toronto Archives**; 45TR, 95R, 96R, © Greg Locke/ **First Light**; 45BL, © Cees Van/**The Stock Market Inc., Toronto**; 45BR, © Wayne Wegner/**First Light**; 51TR, 82–83, **National Ballet of Canada**; 52, © Gilles Benoit/**Hot Shots**; 54, 62L, 106T, © Ron Watts/**First Light**; 56R, Mia & Klaus/**Superstock**; 61TL, 64(both), 98T, 103B, 116TL, 116TR, © Thomas Kitchen/**First Light**; 61TR, 113BR, © Derek Griffiths/**Network Stock Photo File**; 61B, Mary Ellen McQuay/**First Light**; 63L, 106, © Grant Black/**First Light**; 63R, © Milne-Goss/**First Light**; 68, 99TR, 107, © Donald Standfield/**First Light**; 72T, 104I, c Gerda Dillon/**First Light**; 72M, 78T, 109TL, © David Prichard/**First Light**; 74, 78B, 88L, 108, © A. E. Sirulnikoff/**First Light**; 79, 103MB, © Robert W. Allan/**First Light**; 79I, 115TR, 115BR, 116B, © Brian Milne/**First Light**; 81R, 101M, © Lorraine C. Parow/**First Light**; 85T, Courtesy of Susan Schelle; 85R, 85B, **The McMichael Gallery**; 86, © William P. McElligott/**First Light**; 88R, **Mariposa Festival**; 89L, **Opera Hamilton**; 89R, **Toronto Symphony Orchestra**; 90L, Cylla von Tiedemann/**Desrosiers Dance Theatre**; 90R, Cylla von Tiedemann/**Canadian Children's Dance Theatre**; 91, Tom Skudra/**Stratford Festival**; 92L, **Young People's Theatre**; 92R, **Famous People Players**; 93L, Fred Phipps/**CBC**; 93R, Janet Webb/**PWT Photo**; 94L, 113BR, © Barry Griffiths/**Network Stock Photo File**; 96L, © Gary Archibald/**First Light**; 97R, **Athlete's Information Bureau, Ottawa**; 98B, 105L, © Jessie Parker/ **First Light**; 98BL, © Barry Dursley/**First Light**; 104, 113TR, 114TL, 121, © David Scott/**Superstock**; 105R, © Aubrey Diem/**First Light**; 106I, **Jocelyn Smyth**; 109B, © Ken Straiton/**First Light**; 110T, © Walter R. Schmid/**Focus**; 110B, 116I, 123, © L.A. Morse/**The Stock Market Inc., Toronto**; 112TR, © Michael Foster/**Superstock**; 113L, Brian Morin/**Environment Canada, Canadian Parks Service**; 114TR, © Andrew Ptak/**First Light**; 114B, **The Stock Market Inc., Toronto**; 115L, **Superstock**; 117I, © Michelle Burgess/**Superstock**; 126, **The Photo Source/Superstock**; 130T, **Courtesy of the Lieutenant-Governor's Office**; 130MT, **Graeme Gibson**; 132MB, © **Walter Curten, RCA**; 132B, **Nicholas Seiflow**; 133MB, **Brant County Museum**; 134B, **Manitoba Archives**; back cover, © Dennis McColemann/**Focus**